Nonfiction
Reading
Practice

GRADE 1

Reading at ❸ Levels

Writing: Renee Biermann
Content Editing: Barbara Allman
Copy Editing: Laurie Westrich
Art Direction: Yuki Meyer
Art Manager: Kathy Kopp
Cover Design: Yuki Meyer
Illustration: Chris Vallo
Design/Production: Jessica Onken

EMC 3231

Evan-Moor®
Helping Children Learn

Visit
teaching-standards.com
to view a correlation
of this book.
This is a free service.

Correlated to
Current Standards

Congratulations on your purchase of some of the finest teaching materials in the world.

CPSIA: Printed by McNaughton & Gunn, Saline, MI USA. [12/2018]

Contents

What's Inside?

Nonfiction Reading Practice provides 17 units of nonfiction reading selections with topics that span the curriculum. The reading selections progress in difficulty from easiest (Level 1) to hardest (Level 3). Each unit is self-contained and includes materials to provide a rich reading and writing lesson. The contents of each unit is described below.

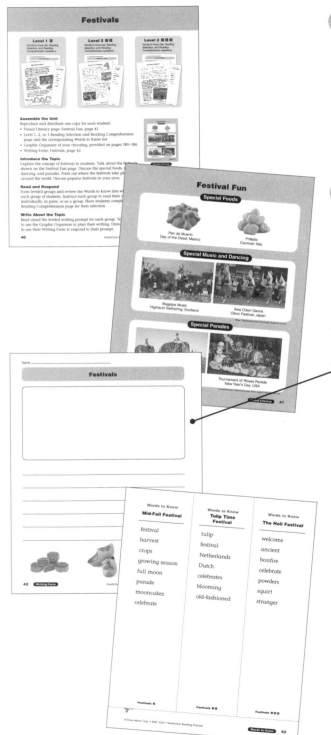

A Teacher Resource Page

A teacher resource page shows unit-specific materials, lists page numbers, and has a suggested teaching path that includes support to introduce the topic.

A Visual Aid

The Visual Literacy page provides information about the topic. This page supports all of the leveled reading selections and is intended to be used as a reference for students in addition to the reading selection.

A Writing Form

The Writing Form is an illustrated page on which students respond to the reading selection–specific writing prompts. The Writing Form in each unit is designed to be used with all three writing prompts.

Vocabulary

The Words to Know lists contain vocabulary for each leveled reading selection. The lists include content vocabulary, phonetically challenging words, and words that may be unfamiliar to students. Words to Know lists must be reproduced and cut apart.

Reading Selections at Three Reading Levels

Each unit presents three reading selections on the same topic. The reading selections progress in difficulty from easiest (Level 1) to hardest (Level 3). An icon indicates the level of the reading selection—Level 1 (▪), Level 2 (▪▪), Level 3 (▪▪▪). Each reading selection contains topic-specific vocabulary and concepts to incorporate into classroom discussion. The Level 1 reading selection gives readers a core vocabulary and a basic understanding of the topic. More challenging vocabulary words are used and additional details are provided as the level of the reading selections increases.

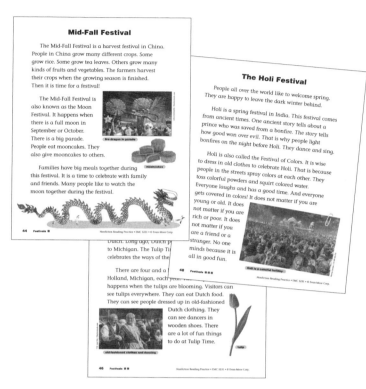

Comprehension Questions

A comprehension page follows each reading selection. There are text-dependent questions in multiple-choice and constructed response formats. The open-ended questions are intended to elicit higher-order thinking skills. As a result, answers will vary.

A Writing Prompt

Write About the Topic, a text-based writing prompt, is given at the bottom of each comprehension page. Students use the Writing Form to write their response. If you plan to display students' writing on a bulletin board, you may wish to have students complete a rough draft on another piece of paper.

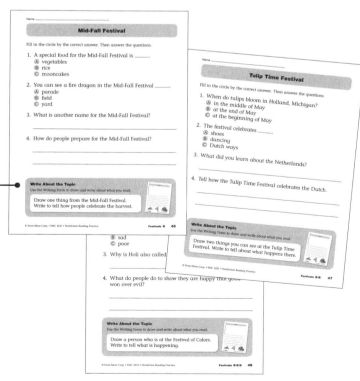

Graphic Organizers

There are seven graphic organizers to help students plan their writing and extend comprehension. The graphic organizers are located on pages 180–186 at the back of the book.

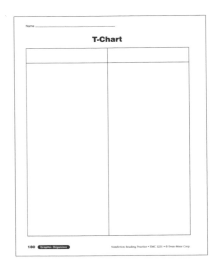

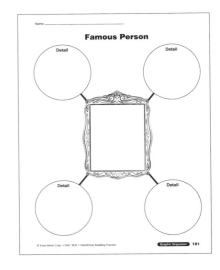

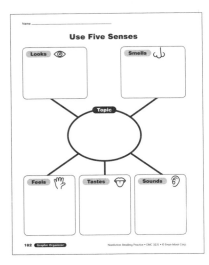

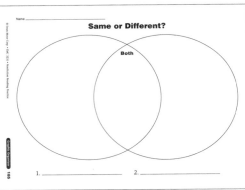

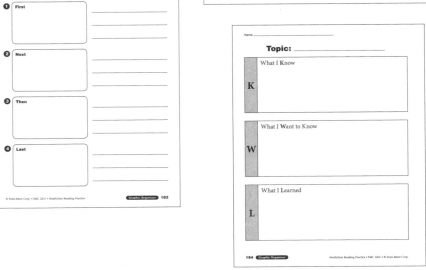

More About *Nonfiction Reading Practice*

Reading Nonfiction Is Important

Research indicates that students are not reading enough nonfiction texts. One reason reading nonfiction is so important is that it helps students develop background knowledge, which accounts for as much as 33 percent of the variance in student achievement (Marzano, 2000). Background knowledge becomes more crucial in the later elementary grades as students begin to read more content-specific textbooks (Young, Moss, & Cornwell, 2007), which often include headings, graphs, charts, and other text elements not often found in the narrative fiction they encountered in the lower grades (Sanacore & Palumbo, 2009).

Readability

All of the reading selections in this series have been edited for readability. Readability formulas, which are mathematical calculations, are considered to be one way of predicting reading ease. The Lexile® Analyzer was used to check for readability. The Lexile® Analyzer measures the complexity of the text by studying its characteristics, such as sentence length, word difficulty, and word frequency. We have used the new Lexile® grade-level spans, as recommended in the Common Core State Standards, to determine where each Lexile® score falls within a grade level.

Planning Instruction

The units in this book do not need to be taught in sequential order. Choose the units that align with your curriculum or with student interests.

- For whole-group instruction, introduce the unit to the whole class. Provide each student with a reading selection at the appropriate reading level. Guide students as they read the reading selections. You may want to have students read with partners. Then conduct a class discussion to share the different information learned.

- For small-group instruction, choose a reading selection at the appropriate reading level for each group. The group reads the reading selection with teacher guidance and discusses the information presented.

- The reading selections may also be used to assist readers in moving from less difficult to more challenging reading material. After building vocabulary and familiarity with the topic at the appropriate level, students may be able to successfully read the reading selection at the next level of difficulty.

Name: _____

Reading Checklist

Before I Read

☐ I think about what I already know.

☐ I think about what I want to learn.

☐ I read the title for clues.

☐ I look at the pictures for clues.

While I Read

☐ I stop and identify the main idea.

☐ I underline important details.

☐ I read the captions below the pictures.

☐ I make pictures of the text in my mind.

☐ I write down questions I have.

☐ I use words I understand to help me figure out words I don't know.

After I Read

☐ I think about the author's purpose.

☐ I speak, draw, and write about what I read.

☐ I reread my favorite parts.

☐ I reread to find details.

☐ I look back at the text to find the answers to questions.

☐ I think about the information I've learned in order to answer questions.

 Nonfiction Reading Practice • EMC 3231 • © Evan-Moor Corp.

Name: _____

My Reading and Writing Record

Write the title of the reading selection you read. Then make a checkmark in the box if you completed the other tasks. Write **yes** or **no** to tell if you liked the topic.

I read...	I answered questions	I planned my writing	I wrote	I liked this topic

A Visit to the Moon

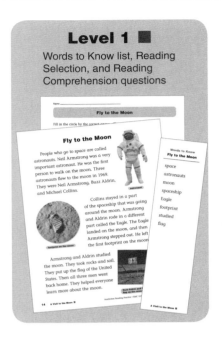
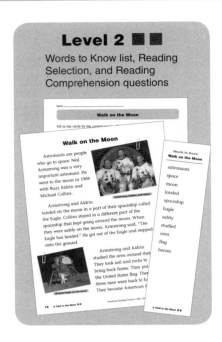
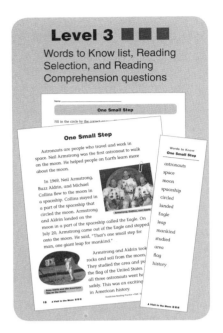
Assemble the Unit

Reproduce and distribute one copy for each student:

- Visual Literacy page: Neil Armstrong Timeline, page 11
- Level 1, 2, or 3 Reading Selection and Reading Comprehension page and the corresponding Words to Know list
- Graphic Organizer of your choosing, provided on pages 180–186
- Writing Form: A Visit to the Moon, page 12

Introduce the Topic

Read aloud and discuss the Neil Armstrong Timeline. Explain that Armstrong was the first person to walk on the moon. Tell students that 12 men from the United States walked on the moon during the years 1969 to 1972.

Read and Respond

Form leveled groups and review the Words to Know lists with each group of students. Instruct each group to read their selection individually, in pairs, or as a group. Have students complete the Reading Comprehension page for their selection.

Write About the Topic

Read aloud the leveled writing prompt for each group. Tell students to use the Graphic Organizer to plan their writing. Direct students to use their Writing Form to respond to their prompt.

Visual Literacy

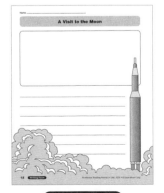

Writing Form

Timeline
Neil Armstrong

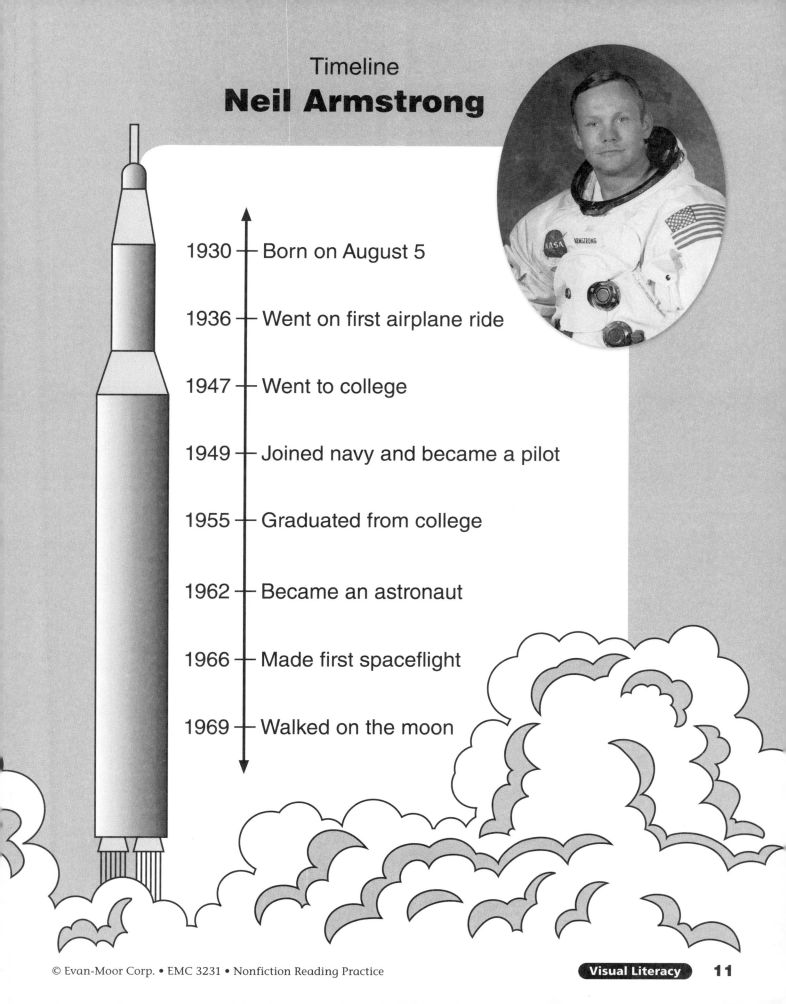

1930 — Born on August 5

1936 — Went on first airplane ride

1947 — Went to college

1949 — Joined navy and became a pilot

1955 — Graduated from college

1962 — Became an astronaut

1966 — Made first spaceflight

1969 — Walked on the moon

A Visit to the Moon

Nonfiction Reading Practice • EMC 3231 • © Evan-Moor Corp.

Words to Know **Fly to the Moon**	Words to Know **Walk on the Moon**	Words to Know **One Small Step**
space	astronauts	astronauts
astronauts	space	space
moon	moon	moon
spaceship	landed	spaceship
Eagle	spaceship	circled
footprint	Eagle	landed
studied	safely	Eagle
flag	studied	leap
	area	mankind
	flag	studied
	heroes	area
		flag
		history

| **A Visit to the Moon** ■ | **A Visit to the Moon** ■ ■ | **A Visit to the Moon** ■ ■ ■ |

Fly to the Moon

astronaut

People who go to space are called astronauts. Neil Armstrong was a very important astronaut. He was the first person to walk on the moon. Three astronauts flew to the moon in 1969. They were Neil Armstrong, Buzz Aldrin, and Michael Collins.

footprint on the moon

Collins stayed in a part of the spaceship that was going around the moon. Armstrong and Aldrin rode in a different part called the Eagle. The Eagle landed on the moon, and then Armstrong stepped out. He left the first footprint on the moon.

Armstrong and Aldrin studied the moon. They took rocks and soil. They put up the flag of the United States. Then all three men went back home. They helped everyone learn more about the moon.

Buzz Aldrin and the American flag on the moon

Fly to the Moon

Fill in the circle by the correct answer. Then answer the questions.

1. Neil Armstrong was the first person to _____.
   Ⓐ go around the moon
   Ⓑ fly in a spaceship
   Ⓒ walk on the moon

2. The three astronauts went to the moon in _____.
   Ⓐ 1969
   Ⓑ 1968
   Ⓒ 1967

3. How did the astronauts help people learn more about the moon?

   _____

4. What was the main idea of the text?

   _____

   _____

Write About the Topic

Use the Writing Form to draw and write about what you read.

Draw Neil Armstrong on the moon.
Write about one thing he did there.

Walk on the Moon

Astronauts are people who go to space. Neil Armstrong was a very important astronaut. He went to the moon in 1969 with Buzz Aldrin and Michael Collins.

Armstrong, Collins, and Aldrin

Armstrong and Aldrin landed on the moon in a part of their spaceship called the Eagle. Collins stayed in a different part of the spaceship that kept going around the moon. When they were safely on the moon, Armstrong said, "The Eagle has landed." He got out of the Eagle and stepped onto the ground.

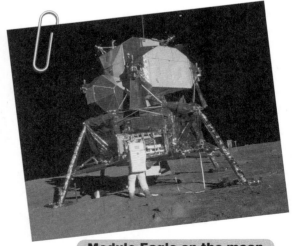

Module Eagle on the moon

Armstrong and Aldrin studied the area around them. They took soil and rocks to bring back home. They put up the United States flag. Then all three men went back to Earth. They became American heroes.

   Nonfiction Reading Practice • EMC 3231 • © Evan-Moor Corp.

Walk on the Moon

Fill in the circle by the correct answer. Then answer the questions.

1. Astronauts are people who _____.
   Ⓐ study space on Earth
   Ⓑ go to space
   Ⓒ study soil and rocks

2. _____ said, "The Eagle has landed."
   Ⓐ Neil Armstrong
   Ⓑ Buzz Aldrin
   Ⓒ Michael Collins

3. What can you learn about astronauts from the photos?

   _____

4. What did Armstrong and Aldrin do on the moon?

   _____

   _____

Write About the Topic
Use the Writing Form to draw and write about what you read.

Draw one of the three astronauts. Write about what that person did in space.

One Small Step

Astronauts are people who travel and work in space. Neil Armstrong was the first astronaut to walk on the moon. He helped people on Earth learn more about the moon.

In 1969, Neil Armstrong, Buzz Aldrin, and Michael Collins flew to the moon in a spaceship. Collins stayed in a part of the spaceship that circled the moon. Armstrong and Aldrin landed on the

Armstrong, Collins, and Aldrin

moon in a part of the spaceship called the Eagle. On July 20, Armstrong came out of the Eagle and stepped onto the moon. He said, "That's one small step for man, one giant leap for mankind."

Buzz Aldrin and the American flag on the moon

Armstrong and Aldrin took rocks and soil from the moon. They studied the area and put up the flag of the United States. Then all three astronauts went home safely. This was an exciting time in American history.

Nonfiction Reading Practice • EMC 3231 • © Evan-Moor Corp.

One Small Step

Fill in the circle by the correct answer. Then answer the questions.

1. Neil Armstrong helped people on Earth _____.
   Ⓐ fly spaceships around the Earth
   Ⓑ learn more about the moon
   Ⓒ walk around on the moon

2. _____ stayed in a part of the spaceship that did not land on the moon.
   Ⓐ Neil Armstrong
   Ⓑ Buzz Aldrin
   Ⓒ Michael Collins

3. What was the surface of the moon like?

   _____

4. What question would you ask Neil Armstrong?

   _____

   _____

Write About the Topic

Use the Writing Form to draw and write about what you read.

Draw Armstrong and Aldrin on the moon.
Write about what they did there.

Learn About History

Level 1 ■
Words to Know list, Reading Selection, and Reading Comprehension questions

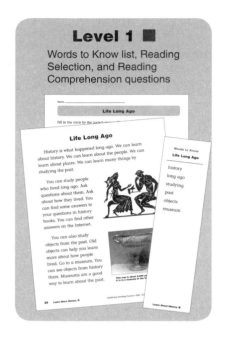

Level 2 ■ ■
Words to Know list, Reading Selection, and Reading Comprehension questions

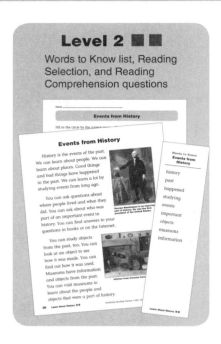

Level 3 ■ ■ ■
Words to Know list, Reading Selection, and Reading Comprehension questions

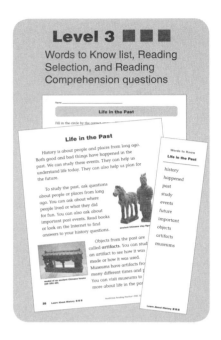

Assemble the Unit

Reproduce and distribute one copy for each student:

- Visual Literacy page: How History Works Timeline, page 21
- Level 1, 2, or 3 Reading Selection and Reading Comprehension page and the corresponding Words to Know list
- Graphic Organizer of your choosing, provided on pages 180–186
- Writing Form: Learn About History, page 22

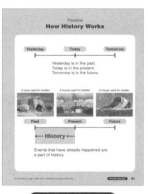

Visual Literacy

Introduce the Topic

Read aloud and discuss the How History Works Timeline. Review the concepts of past, present, and future with students to ensure understanding.

Read and Respond

Form leveled groups and review the Words to Know lists with each group of students. Instruct each group to read their selection individually, in pairs, or as a group. Have students complete the Reading Comprehension page for their selection.

Write About the Topic

Read aloud the leveled writing prompt for each group. Tell students to use the Graphic Organizer to plan their writing. Direct students to use their Writing Form to respond to their prompt.

Writing Form

How History Works

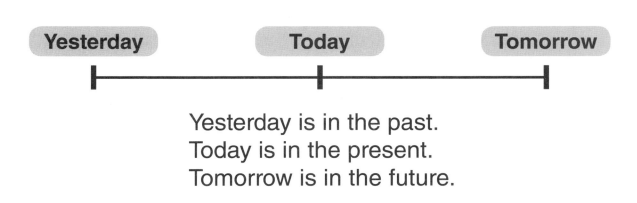

Yesterday   **Today**   **Tomorrow**

Yesterday is in the past.
Today is in the present.
Tomorrow is in the future.

A cave used for shelter.   A house used for shelter.   A house used for shelter.

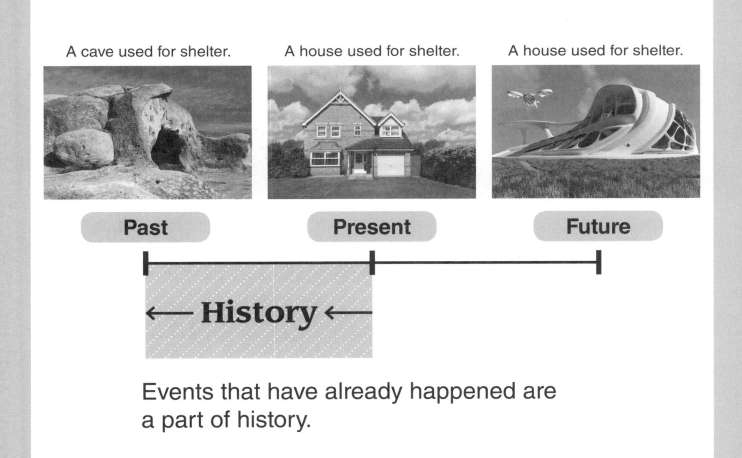

Past   **Present**   **Future**

← **History** ←

Events that have already happened are
a part of history.

Name _____

Learn About History

_____

_____

_____

_____

_____

_____

_____

_____

Words to Know	Words to Know	Words to Know
Life Long Ago	**Events from History**	**Life in the Past**
history	history	history
long ago	past	happened
studying	happened	past
past	studying	study
objects	events	events
museum	important	future
	objects	important
	museums	objects
	information	artifacts
		museums

Life Long Ago

History is what happened long ago. We can learn about history. We can learn about the people. We can learn about places. We can learn many things by studying the past.

You can study people who lived long ago. Ask questions about them. Ask about how they lived. You can find some answers to your questions in history books. You can find other answers on the Internet.

You can also study objects from the past. Old objects can help you learn more about how people lived. Go to a museum. You can see objects from history there. Museums are a good way to learn about the past.

This cup is about 3,000 years old. It is in a museum in the United States.

Name _____

Life Long Ago

Fill in the circle by the correct answer. Then answer the questions.

1. History is what happened in the _____.
   Ⓐ past
   Ⓑ present
   Ⓒ future

2. You can find objects from history in a _____.
   Ⓐ timeline
   Ⓑ new place
   Ⓒ museum

3. What can looking at old objects help you learn?

   _____

4. Tell about one object you can see at a museum.

   _____

   _____

Write About the Topic

Use the Writing Form to write about what you read.

What are two things you can do to learn more about life long ago?

Events from History

History is the events of the past. We can learn about people. We can learn about places. Good things and bad things have happened in the past. We can learn a lot by studying events from long ago.

George Washington is an important part of history. He was the first president of the United States.

You can ask questions about where people lived and what they did. You can ask about who was part of an important event in history. You can find answers to your questions in books or on the Internet.

You can study objects from the past, too. You can look at an object to see how it was made. You can find out how it was used. Museums have information and objects from the past. You can visit museums to learn about the people and objects that were a part of history.

kitchen from Colonial American times

Events from History

Fill in the circle by the correct answer. Then answer the questions.

1. History is about the _____.
   Ⓐ future
   Ⓑ present
   Ⓒ past

2. _____ things have happened in the past.
   Ⓐ Only good
   Ⓑ Only bad
   Ⓒ Both good and bad

3. Who is an important person in United States history?

   _____

4. Do people and places from the past look different from people and places today? Explain your answer.

   _____

   _____

Write About the Topic

Use the Writing Form to write about what you read.

Write three things you can do to learn more about an event from the past.

Life in the Past

History is about people and places from long ago. Both good and bad things have happened in the past. We can study these events. They can help us understand life today. They can also help us plan for the future.

To study the past, ask questions about people or places from long ago. You can ask about where people lived or what they did for fun. You can also ask about important past events. Read books or look on the Internet to find answers to your history questions.

ancient Chinese clay figures

model of an ancient Chinese house (AD 25–220)

Objects from the past are called **artifacts**. You can study an artifact to see how it was made or how it was used. Museums have artifacts from many different times and places. You can visit museums to learn more about life in the past.

Name _____

Life in the Past

Fill in the circle by the correct answer. Then answer the questions.

1. History is about what _____.
   Ⓐ is happening now
   Ⓑ has happened
   Ⓒ will happen

2. You can _____ to learn more about history.
   Ⓐ plan events
   Ⓑ read books
   Ⓒ make artifacts

3. What is an artifact?

   _____

4. What is one artifact you could see at a museum?
   Explain what it shows you about the past.

   _____

   _____

Write About the Topic

Use the Writing Form to write about what you read.

How can you learn more about people from the past?

Maps

Level 1 ▪

Words to Know list, Reading Selection, and Reading Comprehension questions

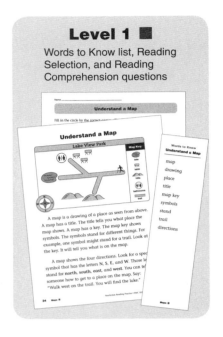

Level 2 ▪▪

Words to Know list, Reading Selection, and Reading Comprehension questions

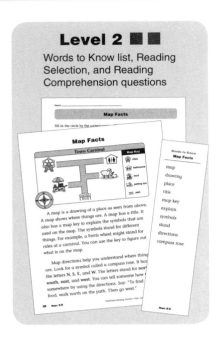

Level 3 ▪▪▪

Words to Know list, Reading Selection, and Reading Comprehension questions

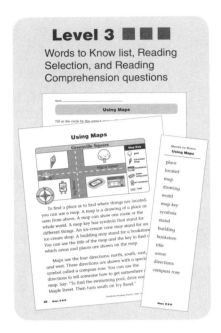

Assemble the Unit

Reproduce and distribute one copy for each student:

- Visual Literacy page: Juan's Neighborhood, page 31
- Level 1, 2, or 3 Reading Selection and Reading Comprehension page and the corresponding Words to Know list
- Graphic Organizer of your choosing, provided on pages 180–186
- Writing Form: Maps, page 32

Introduce the Topic

Review and discuss the features of the map of Juan's Neighborhood with students. Point to locations on the map and have students use the Map Key to identify what they are.

Read and Respond

Form leveled groups and review the Words to Know lists with each group of students. Instruct each group to read their selection individually, in pairs, or as a group. Have students complete the Reading Comprehension page for their selection.

Write About the Topic

Read aloud the leveled writing prompt for each group. Tell students to use the Graphic Organizer to plan their writing. Direct students to use their Writing Form to respond to their prompt.

Visual Literacy

Writing Form

Juan's Neighborhood

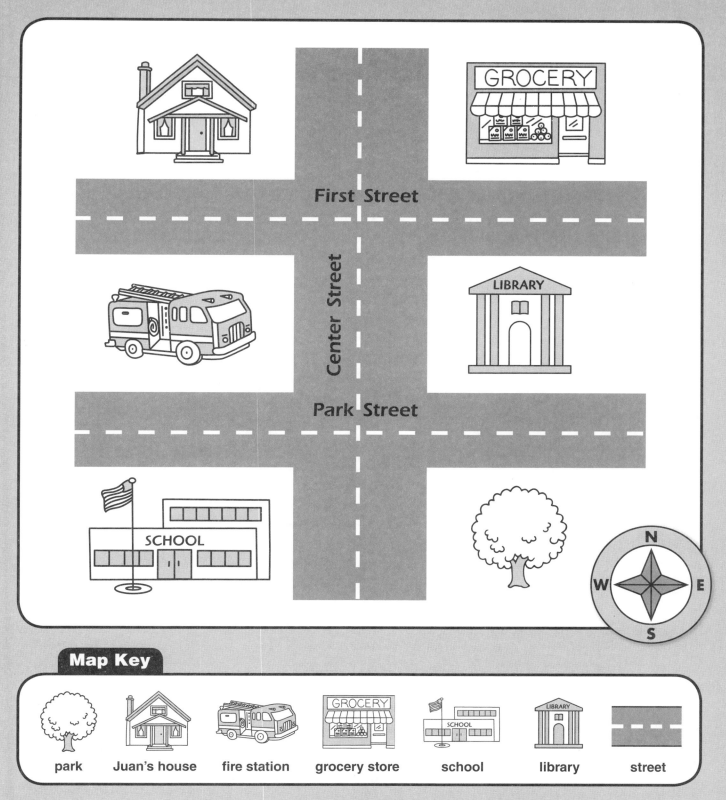

Map Key

| park | Juan's house | fire station | grocery store | school | library | street |

This is a map of Juan's neighborhood.

Name _____

Maps

_____

_____

_____

_____

_____

Nonfiction Reading Practice • EMC 3231 • © Evan-Moor Corp.

Words to Know **Understand a Map**	**Words to Know** **Map Facts**	**Words to Know** **Using Maps**
map	map	place
drawing	drawing	located
place	place	map
title	title	drawing
map key	map key	world
symbols	explain	map key
stand	symbols	symbols
trail	stand	stand
directions	directions	building
	compass rose	bookstore
		title
		areas
		directions
		compass rose
Maps ■	**Maps** ■ ■	**Maps** ■ ■ ■

Understand a Map

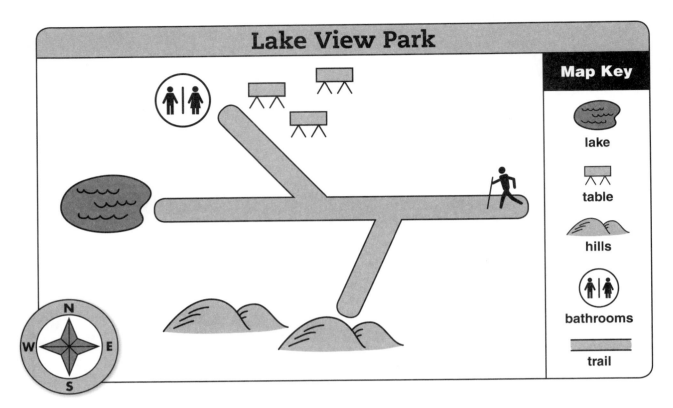

A map is a drawing of a place as seen from above. A map has a title. The title tells you what place the map shows. A map has a key. The map key shows symbols. The symbols stand for different things. For example, one symbol might stand for a trail. Look at the key. It will tell you what is on the map.

A map shows the four directions. Look for a special symbol that has the letters **N**, **S**, **E**, and **W**. Those letters stand for **north**, **south**, **east**, and **west**. You can tell someone how to get to a place on the map. Say: "Walk west on the trail. You will find the lake."

Understand a Map

Fill in the circle by the correct answer. Then answer the questions.

1. A map is a _____ of a place.
   - Ⓐ key
   - Ⓑ symbol
   - Ⓒ drawing

2. A map key has _____ that stand for different things.
   - Ⓐ symbols
   - Ⓑ directions
   - Ⓒ trails

3. How are the four directions shown on a map?

   _____

   _____

4. Imagine you are the person on the trail in Lake View Park. How can you get to the hills?

   _____

   _____

Write About the Topic

Use the Writing Form to draw and write about what you read.

Draw a new symbol to put on the Lake View Park map and key. Write to tell about your symbol.

Map Facts

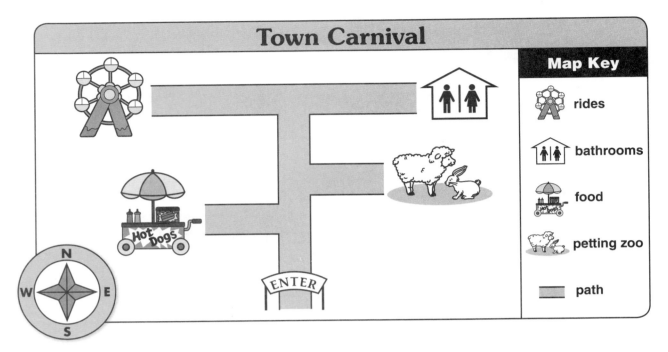

A map is a drawing of a place as seen from above. A map shows where things are. A map has a title. It also has a map key to explain the symbols that are used on the map. The symbols stand for different things. For example, a Ferris wheel might stand for rides at a carnival. You can use the key to figure out what is on the map.

Map directions help you understand where things are. Look for a symbol called a compass rose. It has the letters **N**, **S**, **E**, and **W**. The letters stand for **north**, **south**, **east**, and **west**. You can tell someone how to get somewhere by using the directions. Say: "To find the food, walk north on the path. Then go west."

   Nonfiction Reading Practice • EMC 3231 • © Evan-Moor Corp.

Map Facts

Fill in the circle by the correct answer. Then answer the questions.

1. A map shows _____.
   Ⓐ when something will happen
   Ⓑ how something works
   Ⓒ how a place looks from above

2. A map _____ explains map symbols.
   Ⓐ key
   Ⓑ title
   Ⓒ direction

3. What is the symbol for the food area at the Town Carnival?

   _____

4. What do the letters **N**, **S**, **E**, and **W** stand for?

   _____

Write About the Topic

Use the Writing Form to draw and write about what you read.

Draw your own compass rose. Write why a compass rose is important on a map.

Using Maps

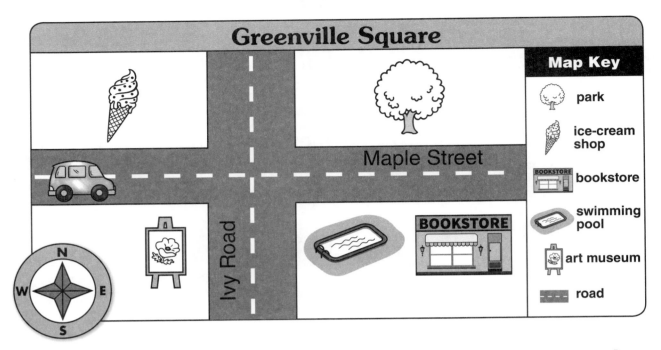

To find a place or to find where things are located, you can use a map. A map is a drawing of a place as seen from above. A map can show one room or the whole world. A map key has symbols that stand for different things. An ice-cream cone may stand for an ice-cream shop. A building may stand for a bookstore. You can use the title of the map and the key to find out which areas and places are shown on the map.

Maps use the four directions: north, south, east, and west. These directions are shown with a special symbol called a compass rose. You can use the directions to tell someone how to get somewhere on the map. Say: "To find the swimming pool, drive east on Maple Street. Then turn south on Ivy Road."

Using Maps

Fill in the circle by the correct answer. Then answer the questions.

1. A map key has _____ that stand for things.
   - Ⓐ directions
   - Ⓑ symbols
   - Ⓒ titles

2. A _____ is a special symbol that shows directions.
   - Ⓐ map key
   - Ⓑ compass rose
   - Ⓒ drawing of a place

3. What is west of the swimming pool in Greenville Square?

   _____

4. What can you use to help you understand a map?

   _____

   _____

Write About the Topic

Use the Writing Form to draw and write about what you read.

Draw a simple map of your classroom. Write directions to tell how to get from the teacher's desk to the door.

Festivals

Level 1 ■

Words to Know list, Reading Selection, and Reading Comprehension questions

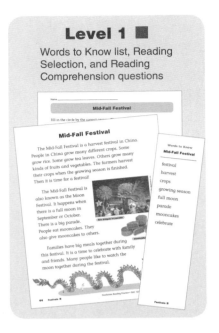

Level 2 ■■

Words to Know list, Reading Selection, and Reading Comprehension questions

Level 3 ■■■

Words to Know list, Reading Selection, and Reading Comprehension questions

Assemble the Unit

Reproduce and distribute one copy for each student:

- Visual Literacy page: Festival Fun, page 41
- Level 1, 2, or 3 Reading Selection and Reading Comprehension page and the corresponding Words to Know list
- Graphic Organizer of your choosing, provided on pages 180–186
- Writing Form: Festivals, page 42

Visual Literacy

Introduce the Topic

Explain the concept of festivals to students. Talk about the festivals shown on the Festival Fun page. Discuss the special foods, music, dancing, and parades. Point out where the festivals take place around the world. Discuss popular festivals in your area.

Read and Respond

Form leveled groups and review the Words to Know lists with each group of students. Instruct each group to read their selection individually, in pairs, or as a group. Have students complete the Reading Comprehension page for their selection.

Writing Form

Write About the Topic

Read aloud the leveled writing prompt for each group. Tell students to use the Graphic Organizer to plan their writing. Direct students to use their Writing Form to respond to their prompt.

Festival Fun

Special Foods

Pan de Muerto
Day of the Dead; Mexico

Frittelle
Carnival; Italy

Special Music and Dancing

Bagpipe Music
Highland Gathering; Scotland

Awa Odori Dance
Obon Festival; Japan

Special Parades

Elephant Parade
Holi Festival of Colors; India

Tournament of Roses Parade
New Year's Day; USA

Festivals

Words to Know	**Words to Know**	**Words to Know**
Mid-Fall Festival	**Tulip Time Festival**	**The Holi Festival**
festival	tulip	welcome
harvest	festival	ancient
crops	Netherlands	bonfire
growing season	Dutch	celebrate
full moon	celebrates	powders
parade	blooming	squirt
mooncakes	old-fashioned	stranger
celebrate		
Festivals ■	**Festivals ■ ■**	**Festivals ■ ■ ■**

Mid-Fall Festival

The Mid-Fall Festival is a harvest festival in China. People in China grow many different crops. Some grow rice. Some grow tea leaves. Others grow many kinds of fruits and vegetables. The farmers harvest their crops when the growing season is finished. Then it is time for a festival!

The Mid-Fall Festival is also known as the Moon Festival. It happens when there is a full moon in September or October. There is a big parade. People eat mooncakes. They also give mooncakes to others.

fire dragon in parade

mooncakes

Families have big meals together during this festival. It is a time to celebrate with family and friends. Many people like to watch the moon together during the festival.

Nonfiction Reading Practice • EMC 3231 • © Evan-Moor Corp.

Mid-Fall Festival

Fill in the circle by the correct answer. Then answer the questions.

1. A special food for the Mid-Fall Festival is _____.
   Ⓐ vegetables
   Ⓑ rice
   Ⓒ mooncakes

2. You can see a fire dragon in the Mid-Fall Festival _____.
   Ⓐ parade
   Ⓑ field
   Ⓒ yard

3. What is another name for the Mid-Fall Festival?

   _____

4. How do people prepare for the Mid-Fall Festival?

   _____

   _____

Write About the Topic

Use the Writing Form to draw and write about what you read.

Draw one thing from the Mid-Fall Festival.
Write to tell how people celebrate the harvest.

Tulip Time Festival

Dutch wooden shoes

The Tulip Time Festival is in Holland, Michigan. It happens every year in the middle of May. The city of Holland is named for a place in the Netherlands. It is known for tulip flowers. It is also known for windmills and wooden shoes. The people who live there are called Dutch. Long ago, Dutch people went to Michigan. The Tulip Time festival celebrates the ways of the Dutch.

Dutch windmill

There are four and a half million tulips grown in Holland, Michigan, each year. The Tulip Time Festival happens when the tulips are blooming. Visitors can see tulips everywhere. They can eat Dutch food. They can see people dressed up in old-fashioned Dutch clothing. They can see dancers in wooden shoes. There are a lot of fun things to do at Tulip Time.

T.W. van Urk / Shutterstock.com

old-fashioned clothes and dancing

tulip

Nonfiction Reading Practice • EMC 3231 • © Evan-Moor Corp.

Name _____

Tulip Time Festival

Fill in the circle by the correct answer. Then answer the questions.

1. When do tulips bloom in Holland, Michigan?
   - Ⓐ in the middle of May
   - Ⓑ at the end of May
   - Ⓒ at the beginning of May

2. The festival celebrates _____.
   - Ⓐ shoes
   - Ⓑ dancing
   - Ⓒ Dutch ways

3. What did you learn about the Netherlands?

   _____

4. Tell how the Tulip Time Festival celebrates the Dutch.

   _____

   _____

Write About the Topic

Use the Writing Form to draw and write about what you read.

Draw two things you can see at the Tulip Time Festival. Write to tell about what happens there.

The Holi Festival

People all over the world like to welcome spring. They are happy to leave the dark winter behind.

Holi is a spring festival in India. This festival comes from ancient times. One ancient story tells about a prince who was saved from a bonfire. The story tells how good won over evil. That is why people light bonfires on the night before Holi. They dance and sing.

Holi is also called the Festival of Colors. It is wise to dress in old clothes to celebrate Holi. That is because people in the streets spray colors at each other. They toss colorful powders and squirt colored water. Everyone laughs and has a good time. And everyone gets covered in colors! It does not matter if you are young or old. It does not matter if you are rich or poor. It does not matter if you are a friend or a stranger. No one minds because it is all in good fun.

Holi is a colorful holiday.

Nonfiction Reading Practice • EMC 3231 • © Evan-Moor Corp.

The Holi Festival

Fill in the circle by the correct answer. Then answer the questions.

1. Holi is a festival where people toss _____.
   Ⓐ rice
   Ⓑ flowers
   Ⓒ powders

2. What do you think the word **wise** means in the text?
   Ⓐ smart
   Ⓑ sad
   Ⓒ poor

3. Why is Holi also called the Festival of Colors?

   _____

4. What do people do to show they are happy that good won over evil?

   _____

   _____

Write About the Topic

Use the Writing Form to draw and write about what you read.

Draw a person who is at the Festival of Colors. Write to tell what is happening.

Matter

Level 1 ■
Words to Know list, Reading Selection, and Reading Comprehension questions

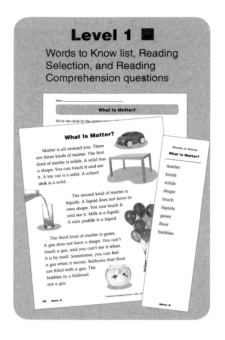

Level 2 ■ ■
Words to Know list, Reading Selection, and Reading Comprehension questions

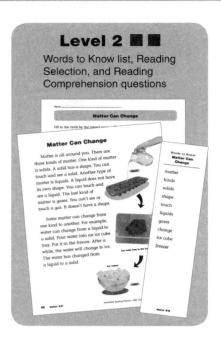

Level 3 ■ ■ ■
Words to Know list, Reading Selection, and Reading Comprehension questions

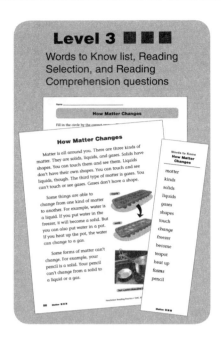

Assemble the Unit

Reproduce and distribute one copy for each student:
- Visual Literacy page: Matter, page 51
- Level 1, 2, or 3 Reading Selection and Reading Comprehension page and the corresponding Words to Know list
- Graphic Organizer of your choosing, provided on pages 180–186
- Writing Form: Matter, page 52

Introduce the Topic

Review and discuss the Matter chart with students. Point to objects in the classroom and have students guess which type of matter each object is. Ask students to explain how they know.

Read and Respond

Form leveled groups and review the Words to Know lists with each group of students. Instruct each group to read their selection individually, in pairs, or as a group. Have students complete the Reading Comprehension page for their selection.

Write About the Topic

Read aloud the leveled writing prompt for each group. Tell students to use the Graphic Organizer to plan their writing. Direct students to use their Writing Form to respond to their prompt.

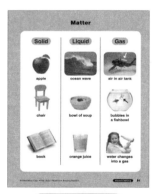

Visual Literacy

Writing Form

Matter

Solid	Liquid	Gas
 apple	 ocean wave	 air in air tank
 chair	 bowl of soup	 bubbles in a fishbowl
 book	 orange juice	 water changes into a gas

Matter

_____

_____

_____

_____

_____

_____

_____

Words to Know	Words to Know	Words to Know
What Is Matter?	**Matter Can Change**	**How Matter Changes**
matter	matter	matter
kinds	kinds	kinds
solids	solids	solids
shape	shape	liquids
touch	touch	gases
liquids	liquids	shapes
gases	gases	touch
float	change	change
bubbles	ice cube	freezer
	freezer	become
		teapot
		heat up
		forms
		pencil
Matter ■	Matter ■ ■	Matter ■ ■ ■

What Is Matter?

Matter is all around you. There are three kinds of matter. The first kind of matter is solids. A solid has a shape. You can touch it and see it. A toy car is a solid. A school desk is a solid.

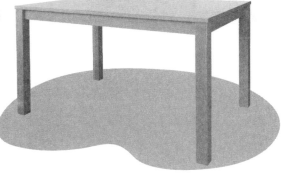

The second kind of matter is liquids. A liquid does not have its own shape. You can touch it and see it. Milk is a liquid. A rain puddle is a liquid.

The third kind of matter is gases. A gas does not have a shape. You can't touch a gas, and you can't see it when it is by itself. Sometimes, you can feel a gas when it moves. Balloons that float are filled with a gas. The bubbles in a fishbowl are a gas.

Name _____

What Is Matter?

Fill in the circle by the correct answer. Then answer the questions.

1. There are _____ kinds of matter.
   - Ⓐ two
   - Ⓑ three
   - Ⓒ four

2. The _____ in a glass of soda are a gas.
   - Ⓐ bubbles
   - Ⓑ liquids
   - Ⓒ shapes

3. Which type of matter has a shape?

   _____

4. What is one kind of liquid?

   _____

Write About the Topic

Use the Writing Form to draw and write about what you read.

Draw a solid, a liquid, or something that has a gas. Tell about the kind of matter you drew.

Matter Can Change

Matter is all around you. There are three kinds of matter. One kind of matter is solids. A solid has a shape. You can touch and see a solid. Another type of matter is liquids. A liquid does not have its own shape. You can touch and see a liquid. The last kind of matter is gases. You can't see or touch a gas. It doesn't have a shape.

Some matter can change from one kind to another. For example, water can change from a liquid to a solid. Pour water into an ice cube tray. Put it in the freezer. After a while, the water will change to ice. The water has changed from a liquid to a solid.

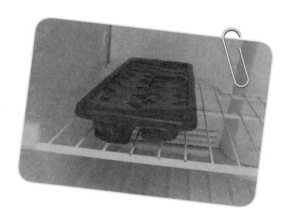

liquid

ice cube tray in the freezer

ice cubes

solid

Nonfiction Reading Practice • EMC 3231 • © Evan-Moor Corp.

Matter Can Change

Fill in the circle by the correct answer. Then answer the questions.

1. Almost everything around you is _____.
   - Ⓐ liquid
   - Ⓑ heated
   - Ⓒ matter

2. _____ is a kind of matter that does not have a shape.
   - Ⓐ A solid
   - Ⓑ An ice cube
   - Ⓒ A gas

3. What kind of matter is water?

   _____

4. How can water change if you put it in the freezer?

   _____

   _____

Write About the Topic

Use the Writing Form to draw and write about what you read.

Draw ice in an ice cube tray. Write to tell about the kind of matter in your picture.

How Matter Changes

Matter is all around you. There are three kinds of matter. They are solids, liquids, and gases. Solids have shapes. You can touch them and see them. Liquids don't have their own shapes. You can touch and see liquids, though. The third type of matter is gases. You can't touch or see gases. Gases don't have a shape.

Some things are able to change from one kind of matter to another. For example, water is a liquid. If you put water in the freezer, it will become a solid. But you can also put water in a pot. If you heat up the pot, the water can change to a gas.

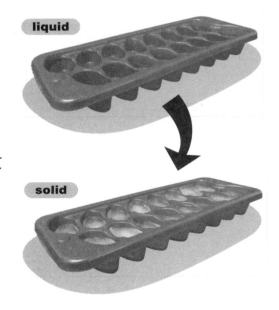

liquid

solid

Some forms of matter can't change. For example, your pencil is a solid. Your pencil can't change from a solid to a liquid or a gas.

hot water changing into a gas

   Nonfiction Reading Practice • EMC 3231 • © Evan-Moor Corp.

How Matter Changes

Fill in the circle by the correct answer. Then answer the questions.

1. _____ are matter that you can't see.
   Ⓐ Solids
   Ⓑ Liquids
   Ⓒ Gases

2. Ice is a _____.
   Ⓐ liquid
   Ⓑ solid
   Ⓒ gas

3. What can happen to water if you heat it in a pot?

   _____

4. Do you have a solid and a liquid in your lunch?
   Write to tell what they are.

   _____

   _____

Write About the Topic

Use the Writing Form to draw and write about what you read.

Draw two ways water can change into a different kind of matter. Write about the changes.

Animal Habitats

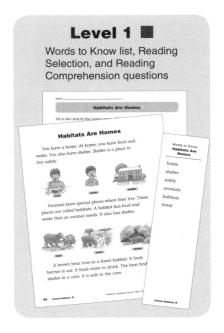

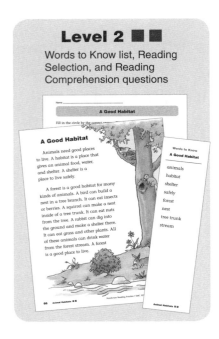

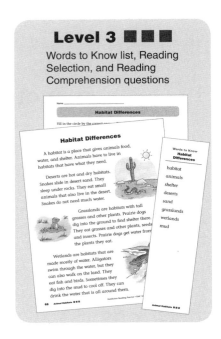

Assemble the Unit

Reproduce and distribute one copy for each student:

- Visual Literacy page: Animal Habitats, page 61
- Level 1, 2, or 3 Reading Selection and Reading Comprehension page and the corresponding Words to Know list
- Graphic Organizer of your choosing, provided on pages 180–186
- Writing Form: Animal Habitats, page 62

Introduce the Topic

Read aloud and discuss the Animal Habitats chart with students. Explain that every animal has a special home, or habitat. Ask volunteers to name an animal from your area. Discuss its habitat.

Read and Respond

Form leveled groups and review the Words to Know lists with each group of students. Instruct each group to read their selection individually, in pairs, or as a group. Have students complete the Reading Comprehension page for their selection.

Write About the Topic

Read aloud the leveled writing prompt for each group. Tell students to use the Graphic Organizer to plan their writing. Direct students to use their Writing Form to respond to their prompt.

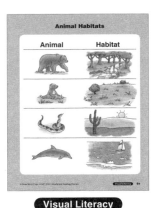

Visual Literacy

Writing Form

Animal Habitats

Animal	Habitat

Animal Habitats

_____
_____
_____
_____
_____
_____
_____

 Nonfiction Reading Practice • EMC 3231 • © Evan-Moor Corp.

Words to Know
Habitats Are Homes

home

shelter

safely

animals

habitats

forest

Animal Habitats ■

Words to Know
A Good Habitat

animals

habitat

shelter

safely

forest

nest

tree trunk

stream

Animal Habitats ■ ■

Words to Know
Habitat Differences

habitat

animals

shelter

deserts

sand

grasslands

wetlands

mud

Animal Habitats ■ ■ ■

Habitats Are Homes

You have a home. At home, you have food and water. You also have shelter. Shelter is a place to live safely.

Animals have special places where they live. These places are called habitats. A habitat has food and water that an animal needs. It also has shelter.

A brown bear lives in a forest habitat. It finds berries to eat. It finds water to drink. The bear finds shelter in a cave. It is safe in the cave.

Habitats Are Homes

Fill in the circle by the correct answer. Then answer the questions.

1. A habitat is _____.
   Ⓐ an animal
   Ⓑ a home
   Ⓒ a berry

2. A shelter is a place where an animal can _____.
   Ⓐ swim in water
   Ⓑ find berries
   Ⓒ live safely

3. What does the brown bear use for shelter?

   _____

4. What do you know about the brown bear's habitat?

   _____

   _____

Write About the Topic

Use the Writing Form to draw and write about what you read.

Draw and write about the things a brown bear needs to live.

A Good Habitat

Animals need good places to live. A habitat is a place that gives an animal food, water, and shelter. A shelter is a place to live safely.

A forest is a good habitat for many kinds of animals. A bird can build a nest in a tree branch. It can eat insects or berries. A squirrel can make a nest inside of a tree trunk. It can eat nuts from the tree. A rabbit can dig into the ground and make a shelter there. It can eat grass and other plants. All of these animals can drink water from the forest stream. A forest is a good place to live.

Name _____

A Good Habitat

Fill in the circle by the correct answer. Then answer the questions.

1. A habitat gives an animal food, water, and _____.
   Ⓐ trees
   Ⓑ nests
   Ⓒ shelter

2. A rabbit can _____.
   Ⓐ make its own shelter
   Ⓑ live without shelter
   Ⓒ eat nuts from trees

3. Why is a forest habitat good for a bird?

   _____

4. What would happen if a forest did not have a stream?

   _____

   _____

Write About the Topic

Use the Writing Form to draw and write about what you read.

Draw a tree in a forest habitat. Write two ways the tree can help animals live.

Habitat Differences

A habitat is a place that gives animals food, water, and shelter. Animals have to live in habitats that have what they need.

Deserts are hot and dry habitats. Snakes slide in desert sand. They sleep under rocks. They eat small animals that also live in the desert. Snakes do not need much water.

Grasslands are habitats with tall grasses and other plants. Prairie dogs dig into the ground to find shelter there. They eat grasses and other plants, seeds, and insects. Prairie dogs get water from the plants they eat.

Wetlands are habitats that are made mostly of water. Alligators swim through the water, but they can also walk on the land. They eat fish and birds. Sometimes they dig into the mud to cool off. They can drink the water that is all around them.

Nonfiction Reading Practice • EMC 3231 • © Evan-Moor Corp.

Name _____

Habitat Differences

Fill in the circle by the correct answer. Then answer the questions.

1. Snakes like habitats that are _____.
   Ⓐ hot and dry
   Ⓑ wet and muddy
   Ⓒ cool and filled with grass

2. Prairie dogs find shelter _____.
   Ⓐ in mud holes
   Ⓑ around desert sand
   Ⓒ under the ground

3. Why are wetlands a good habitat for alligators?

   _____

4. Do animals need a habitat to live? Explain your answer.

   _____

   _____

Write About the Topic

Use the Writing Form to draw and write about what you read.

Draw one of the animals from the text.
Write about its habitat.

Thermometers

Level 1 ■
Words to Know list, Reading Selection, and Reading Comprehension questions

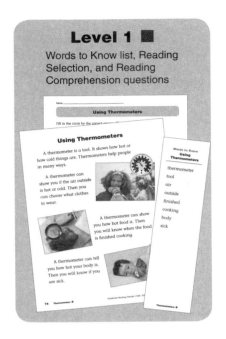

Level 2 ■ ■
Words to Know list, Reading Selection, and Reading Comprehension questions

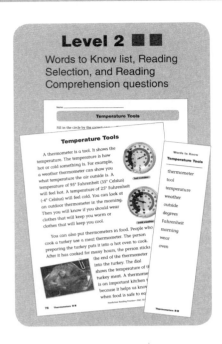

Level 3 ■ ■ ■
Words to Know list, Reading Selection, and Reading Comprehension questions

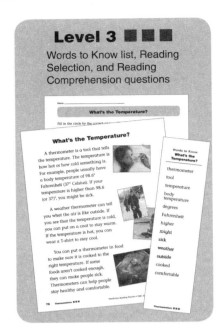

Assemble the Unit
Reproduce and distribute one copy for each student:

- Visual Literacy page: Kinds of Thermometers, page 71
- Level 1, 2, or 3 Reading Selection and Reading Comprehension page and the corresponding Words to Know list
- Graphic Organizer of your choosing, provided on pages 180–186
- Writing Form: Thermometers, page 72

Introduce the Topic
Review each of the thermometers and their names with students. Have students tell where they have seen these types of thermometers before. Discuss how they work.

Read and Respond
Form leveled groups and review the Words to Know lists with each group of students. Instruct each group to read their selection individually, in pairs, or as a group. Have students complete the Reading Comprehension page for their selection.

Write About the Topic
Read aloud the leveled writing prompt for each group. Tell students to use the Graphic Organizer to plan their writing. Direct students to use their Writing Form to respond to their prompt.

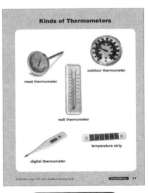

Visual Literacy

Writing Form

Nonfiction Reading Practice • EMC 3231 • © Evan-Moor Corp.

Kinds of Thermometers

meat thermometer

outdoor thermometer

wall thermometer

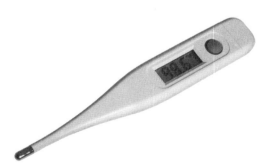

digital thermometer

temperature strip

Thermometers

_____

_____

_____

_____

_____

_____

_____

_____

_____

_____

_____

Words to Know **Using Thermometers**	Words to Know **Temperature Tools**	Words to Know **What's the Temperature?**
thermometer	thermometer	thermometer
tool	tool	tool
air	temperature	temperature
outside	weather	body temperature
finished	outside	degrees
cooking	degrees	Fahrenheit
body	Fahrenheit	higher
sick	morning	might
	wear	sick
	oven	weather
		outside
		cooked
		comfortable
Thermometers ■	**Thermometers** ■ ■	**Thermometers** ■ ■ ■

Using Thermometers

A thermometer is a tool. It shows how hot or how cold things are. Thermometers help people in many ways.

A thermometer can show you if the air outside is hot or cold. Then you can choose what clothes to wear.

A thermometer can show you how hot food is. Then you will know when the food is finished cooking.

A thermometer can tell you how hot your body is. Then you will know if you are sick.

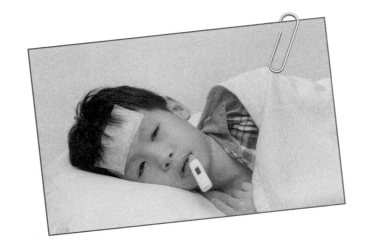

   Nonfiction Reading Practice • EMC 3231 • © Evan-Moor Corp.

Name _____

Using Thermometers

Fill in the circle by the correct answer. Then answer the questions.

1. A thermometer can show you how _____.
   Ⓐ much it rained
   Ⓑ fast the air is moving
   Ⓒ hot or cold the air is

2. A thermometer is a _____.
   Ⓐ tool
   Ⓑ toy
   Ⓒ temperature

3. In what places around a home are thermometers used?

   _____

4. Do people really need to use thermometers? Explain why or why not.

   _____

   _____

Write About the Topic

Use the Writing Form to write about what you read.

Write to tell about two ways you can use a thermometer.

Temperature Tools

A thermometer is a tool. It shows the temperature. The temperature is how hot or cold something is. For example, a weather thermometer can show you what temperature the air outside is. A temperature of 95° Fahrenheit (35° Celsius) will feel hot. A temperature of 25° Fahrenheit (-4° Celsius) will feel cold. You can look at an outdoor thermometer in the morning. Then you will know if you should wear clothes that will keep you warm or clothes that will keep you cool.

hot weather

cold weather

You can also put thermometers in food. People who cook a turkey use a meat thermometer. The person preparing the turkey puts it into a hot oven to cook. After it has cooked for many hours, the person sticks the end of the thermometer into the turkey. The dial shows the temperature of the turkey meat. A thermometer is an important kitchen tool because it helps us know when food is safe to eat.

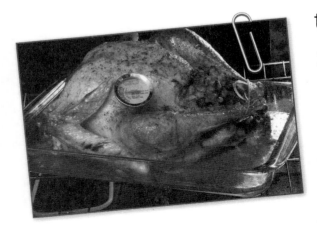

Nonfiction Reading Practice • EMC 3231 • © Evan-Moor Corp.

Temperature Tools

Fill in the circle by the correct answer. Then answer the questions.

1. A thermometer is a kind of _____.
   Ⓐ degree
   Ⓑ temperature
   Ⓒ tool

2. An outdoor thermometer can tell you about _____.
   Ⓐ weather
   Ⓑ candy
   Ⓒ ovens

3. How can a thermometer help you choose what to wear?

   _____

4. Is a meat thermometer different from a weather thermometer? Explain your answer.

   _____

   _____

Write About the Topic

Use the Writing Form to write about what you read.

Describe what a meat thermometer is and how it is used.

What's the Temperature?

A thermometer is a tool that tells the temperature. The temperature is how hot or how cold something is. For example, people usually have a body temperature of 98.6° Fahrenheit (37° Celsius). If your temperature is higher than 98.6° (or 37°), you might be sick.

A weather thermometer can tell you what the air is like outside. If you see that the temperature is cold, you can put on a coat to stay warm. If the temperature is hot, you can wear a T-shirt to stay cool.

You can put a thermometer in food to make sure it is cooked to the right temperature. If some foods aren't cooked enough, they can make people sick. Thermometers can help people stay healthy and comfortable.

Nonfiction Reading Practice • EMC 3231 • © Evan-Moor Corp.

What's the Temperature?

Fill in the circle by the correct answer. Then answer the questions.

1. A tool that tells the temperature is a _____.
   - Ⓐ Fahrenheit
   - Ⓑ degree
   - Ⓒ thermometer

2. You might be _____ if your temperature is higher than 98.6° Fahrenheit (37° Celsius).
   - Ⓐ cold
   - Ⓑ sick
   - Ⓒ comfortable

3. Why should food be cooked to the right temperature?

   _____

4. A weather thermometer shows the temperature of the air. Write the sentence that tells you this.

   _____

   _____

Write About the Topic

Use the Writing Form to write about what you read.

Write to tell how a weather thermometer can help people choose what to wear.

Science Jobs

Level 1 ■
Words to Know list, Reading Selection, and Reading Comprehension questions

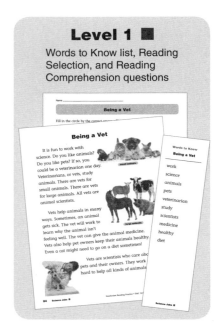

Level 2 ■ ■
Words to Know list, Reading Selection, and Reading Comprehension questions

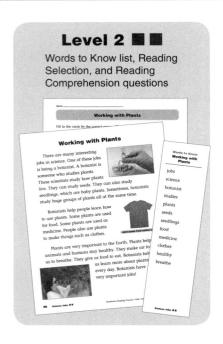

Level 3 ■ ■ ■
Words to Know list, Reading Selection, and Reading Comprehension questions

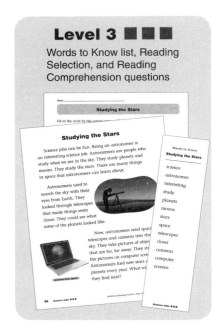

Assemble the Unit

Reproduce and distribute one copy for each student:

- Visual Literacy page: Working with Science, page 81
- Level 1, 2, or 3 Reading Selection and Reading Comprehension page and the corresponding Words to Know list
- Graphic Organizer of your choosing, provided on pages 180–186
- Writing Form: Science Jobs, page 82

Visual Literacy

Introduce the Topic

Tell students that there are many different kinds of jobs that use science. Review the images and descriptions of each type of scientist. Ask students if they feel these jobs would be interesting or fun. Prompt them to support their opinions with reasons.

Read and Respond

Form leveled groups and review the Words to Know lists with each group of students. Instruct each group to read their selection individually, in pairs, or as a group. Have students complete the Reading Comprehension page for their selection.

Writing Form

Write About the Topic

Read aloud the leveled writing prompt for each group. Tell students to use the Graphic Organizer to plan their writing. Direct students to use their Writing Form to respond to their prompt.

Working with Science

Ocean Science
oceans, water, animals, plants

Rock Science
rocks, stones, land, minerals

Plant Science
plant life, seeds

Computer Science
computers, code, programs

Dinosaur Science
dinosaurs, bones, fossils

Animal Science
animals, health, medicine

Visual Literacy   **81**

Name _____

Science Jobs

_____

_____

_____

_____

_____

_____

_____

_____

_____

_____

_____

_____

Words to Know **Being a Vet**	Words to Know **Working with Plants**	Words to Know **Studying the Stars**
work	jobs	science
science	science	astronomer
animals	botanist	interesting
pets	studies	study
veterinarian	plants	planets
study	seeds	moons
scientists	seedlings	stars
medicine	food	space
healthy	medicine	telescopes
diet	clothes	closer
	healthy	cameras
	breathe	computer
		screens

Science Jobs ■   Science Jobs ■ ■   Science Jobs ■ ■ ■

Being a Vet

It is fun to work with science. Do you like animals? Do you like pets? If so, you could be a veterinarian one day. Veterinarians, or vets, study animals. There are vets for small animals. There are vets for large animals. All vets are animal scientists.

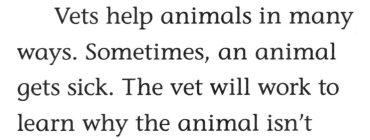

small animals

large animals

Vets help animals in many ways. Sometimes, an animal gets sick. The vet will work to learn why the animal isn't feeling well. The vet can give the animal medicine. Vets also help pet owners keep their animals healthy. Even a cat might need to go on a diet sometimes!

Vets are scientists who care about pets and their owners. They work hard to help all kinds of animals.

Nonfiction Reading Practice • EMC 3231 • © Evan-Moor Corp.

Name _____

Being a Vet

Fill in the circle by the correct answer. Then answer the questions.

1. Veterinarians are scientists who study _____.
   - Ⓐ rocks
   - Ⓑ oceans
   - Ⓒ animals

2. A vet for large animals could _____.
   - Ⓐ give medicine to a horse
   - Ⓑ put a cat on a diet
   - Ⓒ help a sick bird

3. Name two kinds of animals that a vet could help.

   _____

4. What is the main idea of the text?

   _____

   _____

Write About the Topic

Use the Writing Form to write about what you read.

Write to tell what veterinarians do. Would you like to be a vet? Why or why not?

Working with Plants

There are many interesting jobs in science. One of these jobs is being a botanist. A botanist is someone who studies plants.

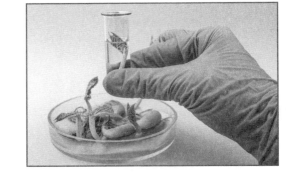

These scientists study how plants live. They can study seeds. They can also study seedlings, which are baby plants. Sometimes, botanists study huge groups of plants all at the same time.

Botanists help people learn how to use plants. Some plants are used for food. Some plants are used as medicine. People also use plants to make things such as clothes.

shirt made from cotton plants

Plants are very important to the Earth. Plants help animals and humans stay healthy. They make air for us to breathe. They give us food to eat. Botanists help us learn more about plants every day. Botanists have very important jobs!

Nonfiction Reading Practice • EMC 3231 • © Evan-Moor Corp.

Working with Plants

Fill in the circle by the correct answer. Then answer the questions.

1. A botanist is someone who studies _____.
   - Ⓐ scientists
   - Ⓑ plants
   - Ⓒ animals

2. A shirt can be made from _____ plants.
   - Ⓐ corn
   - Ⓑ air
   - Ⓒ cotton

3. What is one thing plants can do for people?

   _____

4. What is the main idea of the text?

   _____

   _____

Write About the Topic

Use the Writing Form to write about what you read.

Write to tell what botanists do. Would you like to be a botanist? Why or why not?

Studying the Stars

Science jobs can be fun. Being an astronomer is an interesting science job. Astronomers are people who study what we see in the sky. They study planets and moons. They study the stars. There are many things in space that astronomers can learn about.

Astronomers used to search the sky with their eyes from Earth. They looked through telescopes that made things seem closer. They could see what some of the planets looked like.

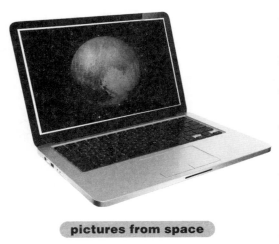

pictures from space

Now, astronomers send space telescopes and cameras into the sky. They take pictures of objects that are far, far away. They study the pictures on computer screens. Astronomers find new stars and planets every year. What will they find next?

   Nonfiction Reading Practice • EMC 3231 • © Evan-Moor Corp.

Studying the Stars

Fill in the circle by the correct answer. Then answer the questions.

1. Astronomers study things that are in _____.
   Ⓐ cameras
   Ⓑ the sky
   Ⓒ Earth

2. Telescopes can make planets look _____.
   Ⓐ closer
   Ⓑ louder
   Ⓒ older

3. Name two types of things an astronomer studies.

   _____

4. What tools do astronomers use today?

   _____

   _____

Write About the Topic

Use the Writing Form to write about what you read.

Write to tell what astronomers do. Would you like to be an astronomer? Why or why not?

Patterns

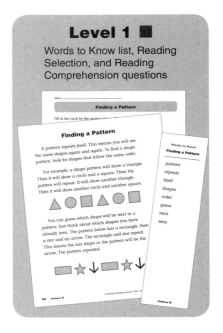
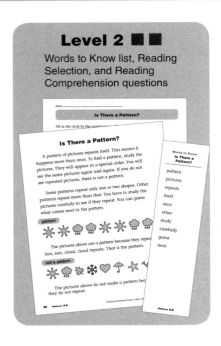
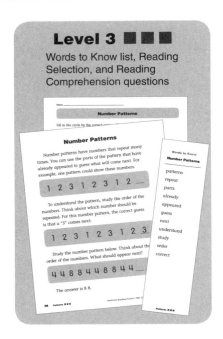
Assemble the Unit

Reproduce and distribute one copy for each student:

- Visual Literacy page: Kinds of Patterns, page 91
- Level 1, 2, or 3 Reading Selection and Reading Comprehension page and the corresponding Words to Know list
- Graphic Organizer of your choosing, provided on pages 180–186
- Writing Form: Patterns, page 92

Introduce the Topic

Review the patterns with students. Echo read each line of the patterns by pointing to a shape, saying its name aloud, and having students repeat. Discuss how the patterns work.

Read and Respond

Form leveled groups and review the Words to Know lists with each group of students. Instruct each group to read their selection individually, in pairs, or as a group. Have students complete the Reading Comprehension page for their selection.

Write About the Topic

Read aloud the leveled writing prompt for each group. Tell students to use the Graphic Organizer to plan their writing. Direct students to use their Writing Form to respond to their prompt.

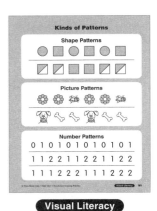

Visual Literacy

Writing Form

Kinds of Patterns

Shape Patterns

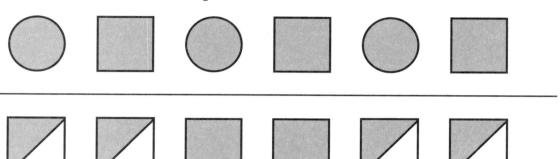

Picture Patterns

Number Patterns

0 1 0 1 0 1 0 1 0 1 0 1 0 1 0 1 0 1

1 1 2 2 1 1 2 2 1 1 2 2 1 1 2 2

1 1 1 2 2 2 1 1 1 2 2 2

Name _____

Patterns

_____

_____

_____

_____

_____

_____

Nonfiction Reading Practice • EMC 3231 • © Evan-Moor Corp.

Words to Know

Finding a Pattern

pattern
repeats
itself
shapes
order
guess
next
seen

Patterns ■

Words to Know

Is There a Pattern?

pattern
pictures
repeats
itself
once
other
study
carefully
guess
next

Patterns ■ ■

Words to Know

Number Patterns

patterns
repeat
parts
already
appeared
guess
next
understand
study
order
correct

Patterns ■ ■ ■

Finding a Pattern

A pattern repeats itself. This means you will see the same shapes again and again. To find a shape pattern, look for shapes that follow the same order.

For example, a shape pattern will show a triangle. Then it will show a circle and a square. Then the pattern will repeat. It will show another triangle. Then it will show another circle and another square.

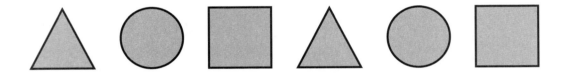

You can guess which shape will be next in a pattern. Just think about which shapes you have already seen. The pattern below has a rectangle, then a star and an arrow. The rectangle and star repeat. This means the last shape in the pattern will be the arrow. The pattern repeated.

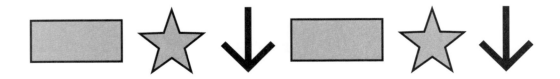

   Nonfiction Reading Practice • EMC 3231 • © Evan-Moor Corp.

Name _____

Finding a Pattern

Fill in the circle by the correct answer. Then answer the questions.

1. A shape pattern shows shapes that _____.
   - Ⓐ only happen once
   - Ⓑ repeat at least once
   - Ⓒ do not appear in order

2. What do you think the word **repeat** means in the text?
   - Ⓐ to happen one time
   - Ⓑ to happen again
   - Ⓒ to happen only two times

3. How can you guess what will happen next in a pattern?

   _____

4. Do shapes make a pattern if they do not follow the same order? Explain your answer.

   _____

   _____

Write About the Topic

Use the Writing Form to draw and write about what you read.

Draw your own shape pattern. Write to tell about your shapes. How do they show a pattern?

Is There a Pattern?

A pattern of pictures repeats itself. This means it happens more than once. To find a pattern, study the pictures. They will appear in a special order. You will see the same pictures again and again. If you do not see repeated pictures, there is not a pattern.

Some patterns repeat only one or two shapes. Other patterns repeat more than that. You have to study the pictures carefully to see if they repeat. You can guess what comes next in the pattern.

pattern

The pictures above are a pattern because they repeat. Sun, sun, cloud, cloud repeats. That is the pattern.

not a pattern

The pictures above do not make a pattern because they do not repeat.

Is There a Pattern?

Fill in the circle by the correct answer. Then answer the questions.

1. The word **repeat** means _____.
   - Ⓐ to happen only once
   - Ⓑ to happen only twice
   - Ⓒ to happen more than once

2. Patterns can have _____.
   - Ⓐ only one picture
   - Ⓑ all different pictures
   - Ⓒ pictures that have a special order

3. When is a group of pictures <u>not</u> a pattern?

   _____

4. What is the main idea of the text?

   _____

   _____

Write About the Topic

Use the Writing Form to draw and write about what you read.

Draw a new picture pattern. Write to tell about patterns and how you can find them.

Number Patterns

Number patterns have numbers that repeat many times. You can use the parts of the pattern that have already appeared to guess what will come next. For example, one pattern could show these numbers:

1 2 3 1 2 3 1 2 ___

To understand the pattern, study the order of the numbers. Think about which number should be repeated. For this number pattern, the correct guess is that a "3" comes next:

1 2 3 1 2 3 1 2 <u>3</u>

Study the number pattern below. Think about the order of the numbers. What should appear next?

4 4 8 8 4 4 8 8 4 4 ___ ___

The answer is 8 8.

          Nonfiction Reading Practice • EMC 3231 • © Evan-Moor Corp.

Number Patterns

Fill in the circle by the correct answer. Then answer the questions.

1. A number pattern shows the same numbers _____.
   - Ⓐ only one time
   - Ⓑ in many different ways
   - Ⓒ more than once in the same order

2. You can study the _____ of the numbers to understand a number pattern.
   - Ⓐ shapes
   - Ⓑ order
   - Ⓒ total

3. What can you do to guess what comes next in a pattern?

   _____

4. Why is a "3" the correct guess for the next number in the first pattern?

   _____

Write About the Topic

Use the Writing Form to draw and write about what you read.

Write your own number pattern. Write to explain why it's a pattern and what comes next.

Money

Level 1 ■
Words to Know list, Reading Selection, and Reading Comprehension questions

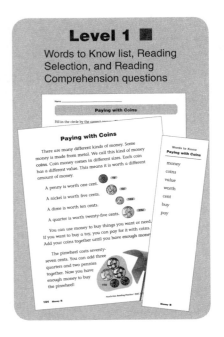

Level 2 ■ ■
Words to Know list, Reading Selection, and Reading Comprehension questions

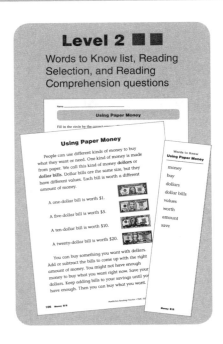

Level 3 ■ ■ ■
Words to Know list, Reading Selection, and Reading Comprehension questions

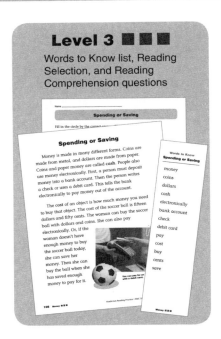

Assemble the Unit

Reproduce and distribute one copy for each student:

- Visual Literacy page: Kinds of Money, page 101
- Level 1, 2, or 3 Reading Selection and Reading Comprehension page and the corresponding Words to Know list
- Graphic Organizer of your choosing, provided on pages 180–186
- Writing Form: Money, page 102

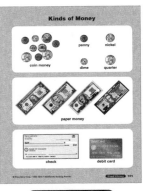

Visual Literacy

Introduce the Topic

Explain that people use money to pay for things. Review each type of money with students. Ask them to share which type of money they are most familiar with.

Read and Respond

Form leveled groups and review the Words to Know lists with each group of students. Instruct each group to read their selection individually, in pairs, or as a group. Have students complete the Reading Comprehension page for their selection.

Write About the Topic

Read aloud the leveled writing prompt for each group. Tell students to use the Graphic Organizer to plan their writing. Direct students to use their Writing Form to respond to their prompt.

Writing Form

Nonfiction Reading Practice • EMC 3231 • © Evan-Moor Corp.

Kinds of Money

coin money

penny

nickel

dime

quarter

paper money

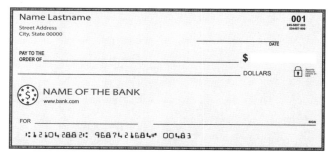

check

debit card

Name _____

Money

_____

_____

_____

_____

_____

_____

_____

_____

_____

_____

_____

Words to Know **Paying with Coins**	Words to Know **Using Paper Money**	Words to Know **Spending or Saving**
money	money	money
coins	buy	coins
value	dollars	dollars
worth	dollar bills	cash
cent	values	electronically
buy	worth	bank account
pay	amount	check
	save	debit card
		pay
		cost
		buy
		cents
		save
Money ■	**Money ■ ■**	**Money ■ ■ ■**

Paying with Coins

There are many different kinds of money. Some money is made from metal. We call this kind of money **coins**. Coin money comes in different sizes. Each coin has a different value. This means it is worth a different amount of money.

A penny is worth one cent.

1¢

A nickel is worth five cents.

5¢

A dime is worth ten cents.

10¢

A quarter is worth twenty-five cents.

25¢

You can use money to buy things you want or need. If you want to buy a toy, you can pay for it with coins. Add your coins together until you have enough money.

The pinwheel costs seventy-seven cents. You can add three quarters and two pennies together. Now you have enough money to buy the pinwheel!

77¢

Name _____

Paying with Coins

Fill in the circle by the correct answer. Then answer the questions.

1. A nickel is made from _____.
   Ⓐ money
   Ⓑ dimes
   Ⓒ metal

2. A _____ is a coin worth twenty-five cents.
   Ⓐ penny
   Ⓑ quarter
   Ⓒ nickel

3. How can you use coins to buy something you want?

   _____

4. Write three facts about coins.

   _____

   _____

Write About the Topic

Use the Writing Form to write about what you read.

Explain what coins are and how they are used.

Using Paper Money

People can use different kinds of money to buy what they want or need. One kind of money is made from paper. We call this kind of money **dollars** or **dollar bills**. Dollar bills are the same size, but they have different values. Each bill is worth a different amount of money.

A one-dollar bill is worth $1.

A five-dollar bill is worth $5.

A ten-dollar bill is worth $10.

A twenty-dollar bill is worth $20.

You can buy something you want with dollars. Add or subtract the bills to come up with the right amount of money. You might not have enough money to buy what you want right now. Save your dollars. Keep adding bills to your savings until you have enough. Then you can buy what you want.

Nonfiction Reading Practice • EMC 3231 • © Evan-Moor Corp.

Using Paper Money

Fill in the circle by the correct answer. Then answer the questions.

1. Dollar bills are paper money that _____.
   - Ⓐ all have different values
   - Ⓑ are all worth five dollars
   - Ⓒ are made in different shapes

2. You can write **ten dollars** as _____.
   - Ⓐ $1
   - Ⓑ $5
   - Ⓒ $10

3. What do people use dollars for?

   _____

4. Write three facts about dollar bills.

   _____

   _____

Write About the Topic

Use the Writing Form to write about what you read.

Explain what dollar bills are and how they are used.

Spending or Saving

Money is made in many different forms. Coins are made from metal, and dollars are made from paper. Coins and paper money are called **cash**. People also use money electronically. First, a person must deposit money into a bank account. Then the person writes a check or uses a debit card. This tells the bank electronically to pay money out of the account.

The **cost** of an object is how much money you need to buy that object. The cost of the soccer ball is fifteen dollars and fifty cents. The woman can buy the soccer ball with dollars and coins. She can also pay electronically. Or, if the woman doesn't have enough money to buy the soccer ball today, she can save her money. Then she can buy the ball when she has saved enough money to pay for it.

You can pay for an item with a debit card.

Nonfiction Reading Practice • EMC 3231 • © Evan-Moor Corp.

Spending or Saving

Fill in the circle by the correct answer. Then answer the questions.

1. Coins can also be called _____.
   - Ⓐ cash
   - Ⓑ paper
   - Ⓒ cards

2. A debit card takes money out of a _____.
   - Ⓐ glass jar
   - Ⓑ sports store
   - Ⓒ bank account

3. How can people pay for something electronically?

   _____

4. How much money does the woman need to buy the soccer ball?

   _____

   _____

Write About the Topic

Use the Writing Form to write about what you read.

Explain three different forms of money.

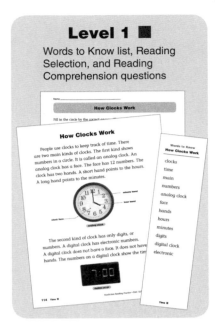

Level 1 ■

Words to Know list, Reading Selection, and Reading Comprehension questions

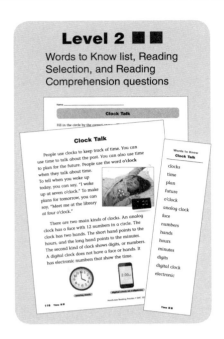

Level 2 ■ ■

Words to Know list, Reading Selection, and Reading Comprehension questions

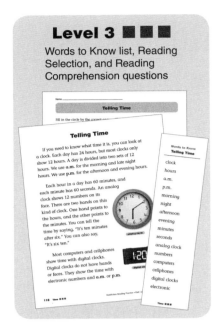

Level 3 ■ ■ ■

Words to Know list, Reading Selection, and Reading Comprehension questions

Assemble the Unit

Reproduce and distribute one copy for each student:

- Visual Literacy page: Kinds of Clocks, page 111
- Level 1, 2, or 3 Reading Selection and Reading Comprehension page and the corresponding Words to Know list
- Graphic Organizer of your choosing, provided on pages 180–186
- Writing Form: Time, page 112

Introduce the Topic

Begin by pointing out your classroom clock and telling its current time. Then review each of the clocks and their names. Discuss with students which types of clocks they use the most in their everyday lives.

Read and Respond

Form leveled groups and review the Words to Know lists with each group of students. Instruct each group to read their selection individually, in pairs, or as a group. Have students complete the Reading Comprehension page for their selection.

Write About the Topic

Read aloud the leveled writing prompt for each group. Tell students to use the Graphic Organizer to plan their writing. Direct students to use their Writing Form to respond to their prompt.

Visual Literacy

Writing Form

Kinds of Clocks

analog clock

cellphone clock

digital clock

cuckoo clock

mantel clock

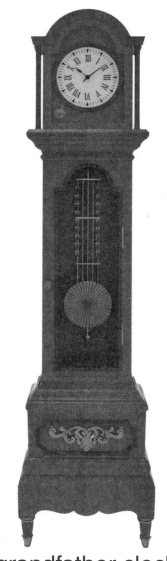

grandfather clock

wristwatch

Name _____

Time

_____

_____

_____

_____

_____

_____

_____

_____

_____

_____

_____

Words to Know	Words to Know	Words to Know
How Clocks Work	**Clock Talk**	**Telling Time**
clocks	clocks	clock
time	time	hours
main	plan	a.m.
numbers	future	p.m.
analog clock	o'clock	morning
face	analog clock	night
hands	face	afternoon
hours	numbers	evening
minutes	hands	minutes
digits	hours	seconds
digital clock	minutes	analog clock
electronic	digits	numbers
	digital clock	computers
	electronic	cellphones
		digital clocks
		electronic
Time ■	Time ■ ■	Time ■ ■ ■

How Clocks Work

People use clocks to keep track of time. There are two main kinds of clocks. The first kind shows numbers in a circle. It is called an analog clock. An analog clock has a face. The face has 12 numbers. The clock has two hands. A short hand points to the hours. A long hand points to the minutes.

analog clock

The second kind of clock has only digits, or numbers. A digital clock has electronic numbers. A digital clock does not have a face. It does not have hands. The numbers on a digital clock show the time.

digital clock

Nonfiction Reading Practice • EMC 3231 • © Evan-Moor Corp.

How Clocks Work

Fill in the circle by the correct answer. Then answer the questions.

1. People can use _____ to keep track of time.
   - Ⓐ an hour
   - Ⓑ a face
   - Ⓒ a clock

2. An analog clock uses _____ to show hours.
   - Ⓐ a small circle
   - Ⓑ a short hand
   - Ⓒ an electronic number

3. How are analog clocks and digital clocks alike?

   _____

4. What is the main idea of the text?

   _____

   _____

Write About the Topic

Use the Writing Form to write about what you read.

Tell what time it is on each of the clocks.
Explain how each clock shows you the time.

Clock Talk

People use clocks to keep track of time. You can use time to talk about the past. You can also use time to plan for the future. People use the word **o'clock** when they talk about time. To tell when you woke up today, you can say, "I woke up at seven o'clock." To make plans for tomorrow, you can say, "Meet me at the library at four o'clock."

There are two main kinds of clocks. An analog clock has a face with 12 numbers in a circle. The clock has two hands. The short hand points to the hours, and the long hand points to the minutes. The second kind of clock shows digits, or numbers. A digital clock does not have a face or hands. It has electronic numbers that show the time.

analog clock

digital clock on cellphone

Nonfiction Reading Practice • EMC 3231 • © Evan-Moor Corp.

Clock Talk

Fill in the circle by the correct answer. Then answer the questions.

1. To talk about time, people use the word _____.
   Ⓐ track
   Ⓑ library
   Ⓒ o'clock

2. You can use time to tell people _____.
   Ⓐ when to meet you somewhere
   Ⓑ what day of the week it is
   Ⓒ which kind of clock to use

3. What does each hand on an analog clock point to?

   _____

   _____

4. How does a digital clock work?

   _____

Write About the Topic

Use the Writing Form to write about what you read.

Write to tell how analog clocks and digital clocks are different.

Telling Time

If you need to know what time it is, you can look at a clock. Each day has 24 hours, but most clocks only show 12 hours. A day is divided into two sets of 12 hours. We use **a.m.** for the morning and late night hours. We use **p.m.** for the afternoon and evening hours.

Each hour in a day has 60 minutes, and each minute has 60 seconds. An analog clock shows 12 numbers on its face. There are two hands on this kind of clock. One hand points to the hours, and the other points to the minutes. You can tell the time by saying, "It's ten minutes after six." You can also say, "It's six ten."

analog clock

Most computers and cellphones show time with digital clocks. Digital clocks do not have hands or faces. They show the time with electronic numbers and **a.m.** or **p.m.**

digital clock

   Nonfiction Reading Practice • EMC 3231 • © Evan-Moor Corp.

Telling Time

Fill in the circle by the correct answer. Then answer the questions.

1. One hour has _____ minutes.
   Ⓐ 12
   Ⓑ 24
   Ⓒ 60

2. The hands of an analog clock show _____.
   Ⓐ the hour and minutes
   Ⓑ if it's morning or night
   Ⓒ the date

3. Is it morning or evening if a digital clock shows 9:15 a.m.?

   _____

4. Write two important facts from the text.

   _____

   _____

Write About the Topic

Use the Writing Form to write about what you read.

Write to tell how analog clocks and digital clocks show time.

Inventions

Level 1 ■
Words to Know list, Reading Selection, and Reading Comprehension questions

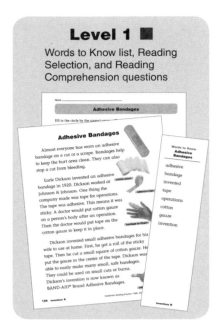

Level 2 ■ ■
Words to Know list, Reading Selection, and Reading Comprehension questions

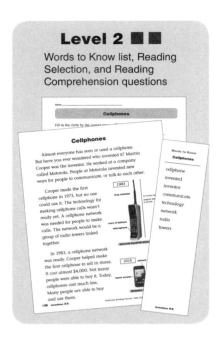

Level 3 ■ ■ ■
Words to Know list, Reading Selection, and Reading Comprehension questions

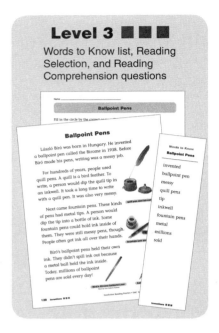

Assemble the Unit

Reproduce and distribute one copy for each student:

- Visual Literacy page: Helpful Inventions, page 121
- Level 1, 2, or 3 Reading Selection and Reading Comprehension page and the corresponding Words to Know list
- Graphic Organizer of your choosing, provided on pages 180–186
- Writing Form: Inventions, page 122

Visual Literacy

Introduce the Topic

Explain to students that an invention is something that has been made for the first time. Discuss how the inventions shown are useful and helpful.

Read and Respond

Form leveled groups and review the Words to Know lists with each group of students. Instruct each group to read their selection individually, in pairs, or as a group. Have students complete the Reading Comprehension page for their selection.

Write About the Topic

Read aloud the leveled writing prompt for each group. Tell students to use the Graphic Organizer to plan their writing. Direct students to use their Writing Form to respond to their prompt.

Writing Form

Nonfiction Reading Practice • EMC 3231 • © Evan-Moor Corp.

Helpful Inventions

paper clips

light bulbs

pencils

scissors

Name _____

Inventions

_____
_____
_____
_____
_____
_____
_____
_____
_____
_____
_____

Words to Know **Adhesive Bandages**	Words to Know **Cellphones**	Words to Know **Ballpoint Pens**
adhesive	cellphone	invented
bandage	invented	ballpoint pen
invented	inventor	messy
tape	communicate	quill pens
operations	technology	tip
cotton	network	inkwell
gauze	radio	fountain pens
invention	towers	metal
		millions
		sold

Inventions ■   Inventions ■ ■   Inventions ■ ■ ■

Adhesive Bandages

Almost everyone has worn an adhesive bandage on a cut or a scrape. Bandages help to keep the hurt area clean. They can also stop a cut from bleeding.

cotton gauze

Earle Dickson invented an adhesive bandage in 1920. Dickson worked at Johnson & Johnson. One thing the company made was tape for operations. The tape was adhesive. This means it was sticky. A doctor would put cotton gauze on a person's body after an operation. Then the doctor would put tape on the cotton gauze to keep it in place.

adhesive tape

bandage on finger

Dickson invented small adhesive bandages for his wife to use at home. First, he got a roll of the sticky tape. Then he cut a small square of cotton gauze. He put the gauze in the center of the tape. Dickson was able to easily make many small, safe bandages. They could be used on small cuts or burns. Dickson's invention is now known as BAND-AID® Brand Adhesive Bandages.

adhesive bandage

Nonfiction Reading Practice • EMC 3231 • © Evan-Moor Corp.

Name _____

Adhesive Bandages

Fill in the circle by the correct answer. Then answer the questions.

1. Earle Dickson used tape that was _____.
   Ⓐ cotton
   Ⓑ sticky
   Ⓒ small

2. Dickson put a piece of cotton _____ on the tape.
   Ⓐ adhesive
   Ⓑ roll
   Ⓒ gauze

3. How could someone use Dickson's bandages?

   _____

4. What is the main idea of the text?

   _____

   _____

Write About the Topic

Use the Writing Form to write about what you read.

Write to tell how Earle Dickson made his invention. Tell why it was helpful.

Cellphones

Almost everyone has seen or used a cellphone. But have you ever wondered who invented it? Martin Cooper was the inventor. He worked at a company called Motorola. People at Motorola invented new ways for people to communicate, or talk to each other.

Cooper made the first cellphone in 1973, but no one could use it. The technology for making cellphone calls wasn't ready yet. A cellphone network was needed for people to make calls. The network would be a group of radio towers linked together.

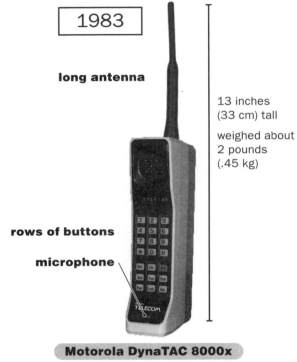

1983

long antenna

13 inches (33 cm) tall

weighed about 2 pounds (.45 kg)

rows of buttons

microphone

Motorola DynaTAC 8000x

In 1983, a cellphone network was ready. Cooper helped make the first cellphone to sell in stores. It cost almost $4,000. Not many people were able to buy it. Today, cellphones cost much less. Many people are able to buy and use them.

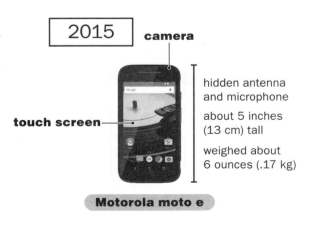

2015

camera

hidden antenna and microphone

about 5 inches (13 cm) tall

weighed about 6 ounces (.17 kg)

touch screen

Motorola moto e

Cellphones

Fill in the circle by the correct answer. Then answer the questions.

1. Martin Cooper invented the first cellphone in _____.
   - Ⓐ 1973
   - Ⓑ 1983
   - Ⓒ 2015

2. Cooper worked at a company called _____.
   - Ⓐ DynaTAC
   - Ⓑ moto e
   - Ⓒ Motorola

3. Why couldn't people use Cooper's first cellphone?

   _____

4. List two facts about the first cellphone sold in stores.

   _____

   _____

Write About the Topic

Use the Writing Form to write about what you read.

Write to tell how cellphones were invented.
Tell what happened in order.

Ballpoint Pens

László Bíró was born in Hungary. He invented a ballpoint pen called the Birome in 1938. Before Bíró made his pens, writing was a messy job.

For hundreds of years, people used quill pens. A quill is a bird feather. To write, a person would dip the quill tip in an inkwell. It took a long time to write with a quill pen. It was also very messy.

quill pen and inkwell

Next came fountain pens. These kinds of pens had metal tips. A person would dip the tip into a bottle of ink. Some fountain pens could hold ink inside of them. They were still messy pens, though. People often got ink all over their hands.

fountain pen and ink bottle

Bíró's ballpoint pens held their own ink. They didn't spill ink out because a metal ball held the ink inside. Today, millions of ballpoint pens are sold every day!

Bíró's Birome ballpoint pen

ballpoint pen today

Photo by User: Roberto Fiadone

Name _____

Ballpoint Pens

Fill in the circle by the correct answer. Then answer the questions.

1. László Bíró invented a _____.
   Ⓐ quill pen
   Ⓑ fountain pen
   Ⓒ ballpoint pen

2. A quill pen is made from a _____.
   Ⓐ metal ball
   Ⓑ real feather
   Ⓒ jar of ink

3. What sentence tells why some people may not like to use fountain pens?

   _____

4. How do you know people today still like using ballpoint pens?

   _____

Write About the Topic

Use the Writing Form to write about what you read.

Write to tell why László Bíró's invention was so useful.

Transportation Technology

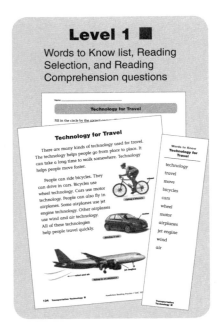

Level 1 ■

Words to Know list, Reading Selection, and Reading Comprehension questions

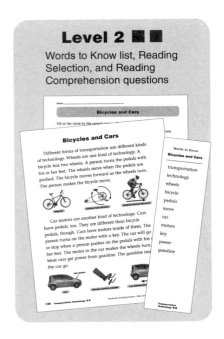

Level 2 ■ ■

Words to Know list, Reading Selection, and Reading Comprehension questions

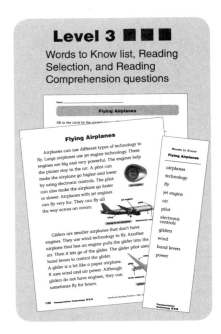

Level 3 ■ ■ ■

Words to Know list, Reading Selection, and Reading Comprehension questions

Assemble the Unit

Reproduce and distribute one copy for each student:

- Visual Literacy page: Kinds of Transportation, page 131
- Level 1, 2, or 3 Reading Selection and Reading Comprehension page and the corresponding Words to Know list
- Graphic Organizer of your choosing, provided on pages 180–186
- Writing Form: Transportation Technology, page 132

Introduce the Topic

Point out and name each type of transportation. Explain to students that each type uses technology to work or move. Ask them which types of transportation they have used before.

Read and Respond

Form leveled groups and review the Words to Know lists with each group of students. Instruct each group to read their selection individually, in pairs, or as a group. Have students complete the Reading Comprehension page for their selection.

Write About the Topic

Read aloud the leveled writing prompt for each group. Tell students to use the Graphic Organizer to plan their writing. Direct students to use their Writing Form to respond to their prompt.

Visual Literacy

Writing Form

Kinds of Transportation

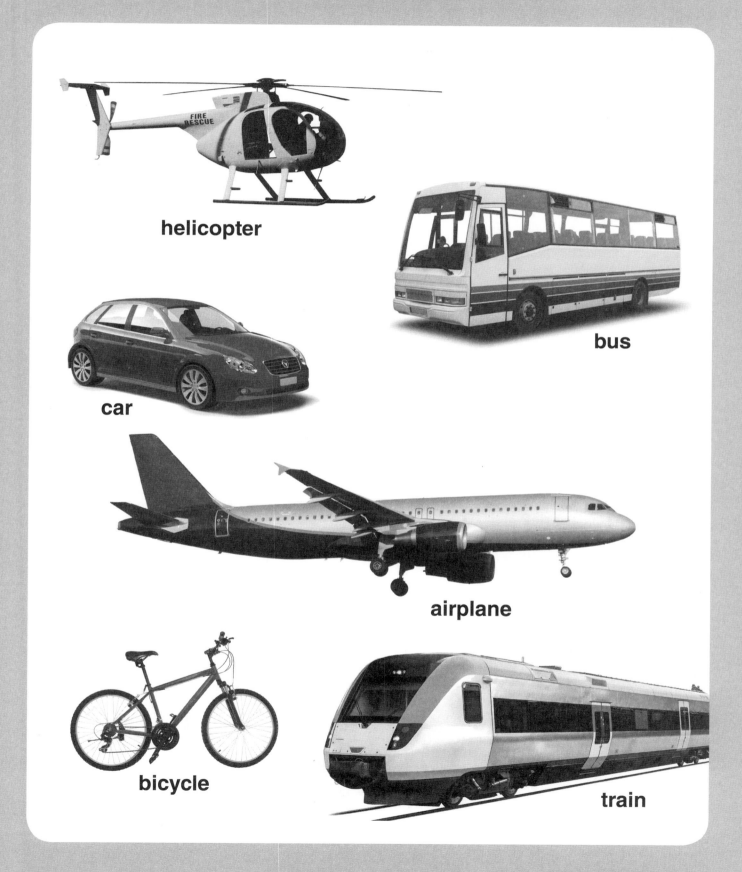

helicopter

bus

car

airplane

bicycle

train

Name _____

Transportation Technology

_____

_____

_____

_____

_____

_____

_____

_____

_____

_____

Words to Know	Words to Know	Words to Know
Technology for Travel	**Bicycles and Cars**	**Flying Airplanes**
technology	transportation	airplanes
travel	technology	technology
move	wheels	fly
bicycles	bicycle	jet engine
cars	pedals	air
wheel	move	pilot
motor	car	electronic controls
airplanes	motors	gliders
jet engine	key	wind
wind	power	hand levers
air	gasoline	power

Words to Know

Technology for Travel

There are many kinds of technology used for travel. The technology helps people go from place to place. It can take a long time to walk somewhere. Technology helps people move faster.

People can ride bicycles. They can drive in cars. Bicycles use wheel technology. Cars use motor technology. People can also fly in airplanes. Some airplanes use jet engine technology. Other airplanes use wind and air technology. All of these technologies help people travel quickly.

wheel

riding a bicycle

motor

driving a car

wind and air

jet engine

flying in an airplane

Name _____

Technology for Travel

Fill in the circle by the correct answer. Then answer the questions.

1. _____ helps people travel more quickly.
    Ⓐ Walking
    Ⓑ Air
    Ⓒ Technology

2. A bicycle moves with _____ technology.
    Ⓐ wheel
    Ⓑ wind
    Ⓒ motor

3. What is one kind of technology that airplanes can use?

    _____

4. Write two reasons from the text that technology is needed for travel.

    _____

    _____

Write About the Topic
Use the Writing Form to write about what you read.

> Write to tell how people can use technology to travel from place to place.

Bicycles and Cars

Different forms of transportation use different kinds of technology. Wheels are one kind of technology. A bicycle has two wheels. A person turns the pedals with his or her feet. The wheels move when the pedals are pushed. The bicycle moves forward as the wheels turn. The person makes the bicycle move.

bicycle

pedals turn wheels

bicycle moves forward

Car motors are another kind of technology. Cars have pedals, too. They are different than bicycle pedals, though. Cars have motors inside of them. The person turns on the motor with a key. The car will go or stop when a person pushes on the pedals with his or her feet. The motor in the car makes the wheels turn. Most cars get power from gasoline. The gasoline makes the car go.

car motor
car

person pushes pedals

car moves forward or backward

Bicycles and Cars

Fill in the circle by the correct answer. Then answer the questions.

1. A person uses his or her _____ to make a bicycle move.
   - Ⓐ hands
   - Ⓑ keys
   - Ⓒ feet

2. Most cars use _____ to get power.
   - Ⓐ gasoline
   - Ⓑ wheels
   - Ⓒ people

3. What kind of technology do cars use?

   _____

4. Are pedals an important part of bicycle and car technology? Explain why or why not.

   _____

   _____

Write About the Topic

Use the Writing Form to write about what you read.

> Write to tell about bicycle and car technologies. Tell how they are alike and different.

Flying Airplanes

Airplanes can use different types of technology to fly. Large airplanes use jet engine technology. These engines are big and very powerful. The engines help the planes stay in the air. A pilot can make the airplane go higher and lower by using electronic controls. The pilot can also make the airplane go faster or slower. Airplanes with jet engines can fly very far. They can fly all the way across an ocean.

jet engine

jet engine

pilot

wing

flying in an airplane

electronic controls

Gliders are smaller airplanes that don't have engines. They use wind technology to fly. Another airplane that has an engine pulls the glider into the air. Then it lets go of the glider. The glider pilot uses hand levers to control the glider. A glider is a lot like a paper airplane. It uses wind and air power. Although gliders do not have engines, they can sometimes fly for hours.

wing

pilot

lever controls

glider flying

 Nonfiction Reading Practice • EMC 3231 • © Evan-Moor Corp.

Name _____

Flying Airplanes

Fill in the circle by the correct answer. Then answer the questions.

1. An airplane that can fly across an ocean uses _____ technology.
   - Ⓐ glider
   - Ⓑ wind
   - Ⓒ jet engine

2. A pilot in a glider uses _____ to control it.
   - Ⓐ electronic controls
   - Ⓑ hand levers
   - Ⓒ engines

3. What kind of technology does a glider use?

   _____

4. How are airplanes and gliders different?

   _____

   _____

Write About the Topic

Use the Writing Form to write about what you read.

Write to tell how jet engine airplanes and gliders use different technology to fly.

E-books

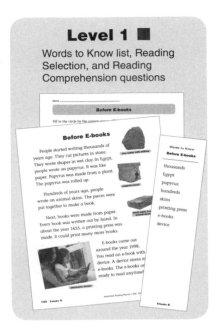

Level 1 ■

Words to Know list, Reading Selection, and Reading Comprehension questions

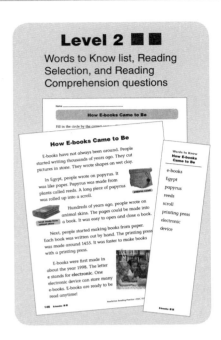

Level 2 ■ ■

Words to Know list, Reading Selection, and Reading Comprehension questions

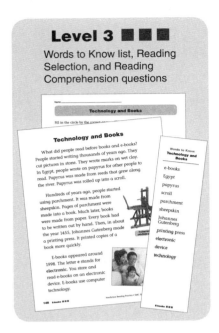

Level 3 ■ ■ ■

Words to Know list, Reading Selection, and Reading Comprehension questions

Assemble the Unit

Reproduce and distribute one copy for each student:

- Visual Literacy page: Books and Writing Timeline, page 141
- Level 1, 2, or 3 Reading Selection and Reading Comprehension page and the corresponding Words to Know list
- Graphic Organizer of your choosing, provided on pages 180–186
- Writing Form: E-books, page 142

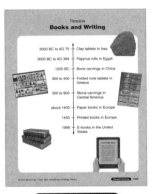

Visual Literacy

Introduce the Topic

Read aloud and discuss the timeline. It gives a history of books and writing. Discuss the images of different types of writing. Ask children if they have seen them before. Where?

Read and Respond

Form leveled groups and review the Words to Know lists with each group of students. Instruct each group to read their selection individually, in pairs, or as a group. Have students complete the Reading Comprehension page for their selection.

Write About the Topic

Read aloud the leveled writing prompt for each group. Tell students to use the Graphic Organizer to plan their writing. Direct students to use their Writing Form to respond to their prompt.

Writing Form

Timeline
Books and Writing

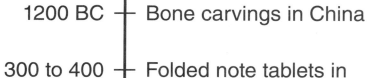

3000 BC to AD 394	Papyrus rolls in Egypt
3000 BC to AD 75	Clay tablets in Iraq
1200 BC	Bone carvings in China
300 to 400	Folded note tablets in Greece
300 to 900	Stone carvings in Central America
about 1400	Paper books in Europe
1455	Printed books in Europe
1998	E-books in the United States

ELECTRONIC BOOK

Name _____

E-books

_____

_____

_____

_____

_____

_____

_____

_____

_____

Words to Know	Words to Know	Words to Know
Before E-books	**How E-books Came to Be**	**Technology and Books**
thousands	e-books	e-books
Egypt	Egypt	Egypt
papyrus	papyrus	papyrus
hundreds	reeds	scroll
skins	scroll	parchment
printing press	printing press	sheepskin
e-books	electronic	Johannes Gutenberg
device	device	printing press
		electronic
		device
		technology
E-books ■	E-books ■ ■	E-books ■ ■ ■

Before E-books

People started writing thousands of years ago. They cut pictures in stone. They wrote shapes in wet clay. In Egypt, people wrote on papyrus. It was like paper. Papyrus was made from a plant. The papyrus was rolled up.

clay tablet with writing

papyrus scroll

Hundreds of years ago, people wrote on animal skins. The pieces were put together to make a book.

book made from animal skins

Next, books were made from paper. Every book was written out by hand. In about the year 1455, a printing press was made. It could print many more books.

electronic device

E-books came out around the year 1998. You read an e-book with a device. A device stores many e-books. The e-books are ready to read anytime!

Nonfiction Reading Practice • EMC 3231 • © Evan-Moor Corp.

Name _____

Before E-books

Fill in the circle by the correct answer. Then answer the questions.

1. People wrote on _____ thousands of years ago.
   - Ⓐ paper
   - Ⓑ animal skins
   - Ⓒ wet clay

2. Today, children can read _____.
   - Ⓐ e-books
   - Ⓑ papyrus
   - Ⓒ marks in clay

3. Pretend you lived hundreds of years ago. What kind of book might you have read?

   _____

   _____

4. Why is a device useful?

   _____

Write About the Topic

Use the Writing Form to write about what you read.

Tell how reading a book was different before and after 1998.

How E-books Came to Be

E-books have not always been around. People started writing thousands of years ago. They cut pictures in stone. They wrote shapes on wet clay.

In Egypt, people wrote on papyrus. It was like paper. Papyrus was made from plants called reeds. A long piece of papyrus was rolled up into a scroll.

papyrus scroll

book made from animal skins

Hundreds of years ago, people wrote on animal skins. The pages could be made into a book. It was easy to open and close a book.

Next, people started making books from paper. Each book was written out by hand. The printing press was made around 1455. It was faster to make books with a printing press.

E-books were first made in about the year 1998. The letter e stands for **electronic**. One electronic device can store many e-books. E-books are ready to be read anytime!

Nonfiction Reading Practice • EMC 3231 • © Evan-Moor Corp.

Name _____

How E-books Came to Be

Fill in the circle by the correct answer. Then answer the questions.

1. Many thousands of years ago _____.
   - Ⓐ people wrote on animal skins
   - Ⓑ people cut pictures in rocks
   - Ⓒ a printing press was made

2. Books were made from _____.
   - Ⓐ wet clay
   - Ⓑ stones
   - Ⓒ animal skins

3. Tell why it would be easier to find your place in a book than a long scroll.

   _____

   _____

4. More books were made after 1455. Why?

   _____

Write About the Topic

Use the Writing Form to write about what you read.

Write to tell how storing e-books is different from storing printed books.

Technology and Books

What did people read before books and e-books? People started writing thousands of years ago. They cut pictures in stone. They wrote marks on wet clay. In Egypt, people wrote on papyrus for other people to read. Papyrus was made from reeds that grew along the river. Papyrus was rolled up into a scroll.

Hundreds of years ago, people started using parchment. It was made from sheepskin. Pages of parchment were made into a book. Much later, books were made from paper. Every book had to be written out by hand. Then, in about the year 1455, Johannes Gutenberg made a printing press. It printed copies of a book more quickly.

Gutenberg's printing press

E-books appeared around 1998. The letter **e** stands for **electronic**. You store and read e-books on an electronic device. E-books use computer technology.

Name _____

Technology and Books

Fill in the circle by the correct answer. Then answer the questions.

1. Gutenberg's machine was _____.
   Ⓐ an electronic device
   Ⓑ a scroll
   Ⓒ a printing press

2. People in Egypt used _____.
   Ⓐ parchment
   Ⓑ papyrus
   Ⓒ computers

3. What is the same about a book and an e-book?

   _____

4. Do you think the people who made books were happy when the printing press was made? Explain your answer.

   _____

   _____

Write About the Topic

Use the Writing Form to write about what you read.

Compare a papyrus scroll and an e-book.
Tell how they are alike and different.

Beatrix Potter

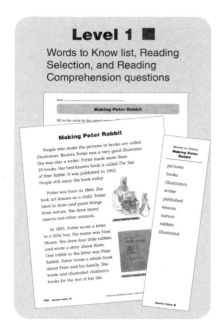

Level 1 ■
Words to Know list, Reading Selection, and Reading Comprehension questions

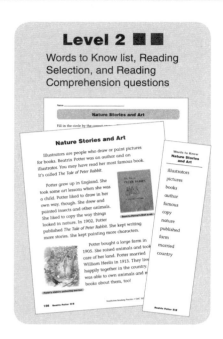

Level 2 ■ ■
Words to Know list, Reading Selection, and Reading Comprehension questions

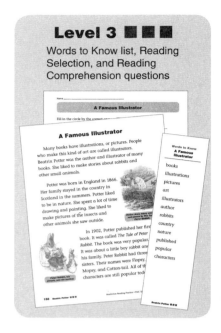

Level 3 ■ ■ ■
Words to Know list, Reading Selection, and Reading Comprehension questions

Assemble the Unit

Reproduce and distribute one copy for each student:

- Visual Literacy page: Beatrix Potter Timeline, page 151
- Level 1, 2, or 3 Reading Selection and Reading Comprehension page and the corresponding Words to Know list
- Graphic Organizer of your choosing, provided on pages 180–186
- Writing Form: Beatrix Potter, page 152

Introduce the Topic

Read aloud and discuss the timeline of Beatrix Potter's life. Explain that she was a painter and a writer. Tell students that Peter Rabbit is a character from Potter's books.

Read and Respond

Form leveled groups and review the Words to Know lists with each group of students. Instruct each group to read their selection individually, in pairs, or as a group. Have students complete the Reading Comprehension page for their selection.

Write About the Topic

Read aloud the leveled writing prompt for each group. Tell students to use the Graphic Organizer to plan their writing. Direct students to use their Writing Form to respond to their prompt.

Visual Literacy

Writing Form

Nonfiction Reading Practice • EMC 3231 • © Evan-Moor Corp.

Timeline
Beatrix Potter

Copyright © 2015 Omar F. A. Gutiérrez Powered by WordPress and Origin

1866 — Born on July 28

1878 — Took art lessons

1860 — Won first art award

1892 — Sold first paintings

1902 — Published *The Tale of Peter Rabbit*

1905 — Bought large farm

1913 — Married William Heelis

1943 — Died at age 77 on December 22

Name _____

Beatrix Potter

Words to Know **Making Peter Rabbit**	Words to Know **Nature Stories and Art**	Words to Know **A Famous Illustrator**
pictures	illustrators	books
books	pictures	illustrations
illustrators	books	pictures
writer	author	art
published	famous	illustrators
lessons	copy	author
nature	nature	rabbits
rabbits	published	country
illustrated	farm	nature
	married	published
	country	popular
		characters

Beatrix Potter ■ | **Beatrix Potter** ■ ■ | **Beatrix Potter** ■ ■ ■

Making Peter Rabbit

People who make the pictures in books are called illustrators. Beatrix Potter was a very good illustrator. She was also a writer. Potter made more than 20 books. Her best-known book is called *The Tale of Peter Rabbit*. It was published in 1902. People still enjoy the book today.

Potter was born in 1866. She took art lessons as a child. Potter liked to draw and paint things from nature. She drew many insects and other animals.

Peter Rabbit's family

In 1893, Potter wrote a letter to a little boy. His name was Noel Moore. She drew four little rabbits and wrote a story about them. One rabbit in the letter was Peter Rabbit. Potter wrote a whole book about Peter and his family. She wrote and illustrated children's books for the rest of her life.

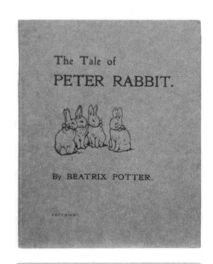

Beatrix Potter's first book

Making Peter Rabbit

Fill in the circle by the correct answer. Then answer the questions.

1. Beatrix Potter was an author and _____.
   - Ⓐ an art teacher
   - Ⓑ an illustrator
   - Ⓒ a nature scientist

2. *The Tale of Peter Rabbit* was published in _____.
   - Ⓐ 1866
   - Ⓑ 1893
   - Ⓒ 1902

3. What makes Peter Rabbit different from real rabbits?

   _____

4. How did *The Tale of Peter Rabbit* come to be?

   _____

   _____

Write About the Topic

Use the Writing Form to draw and write about what you read.

Draw Peter Rabbit. Write to tell three things about Beatrix Potter's life.

Nature Stories and Art

Illustrators are people who draw or paint pictures for books. Beatrix Potter was an author and an illustrator. You may have read her most famous book. It's called *The Tale of Peter Rabbit*.

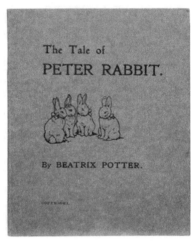

Beatrix Potter's first book

Potter grew up in England. She took some art lessons when she was a child. Potter liked to draw in her own way, though. She drew and painted insects and other animals. She liked to copy the way things looked in nature. In 1902, Potter published *The Tale of Peter Rabbit*. She kept writing more stories. She kept painting more characters.

Peter's sisters gathering berries

Potter bought a large farm in 1905. She raised animals and took care of her land. Potter married William Heelis in 1913. They lived happily together in the country. She was able to own animals and make books about them, too!

Nature Stories and Art

Fill in the circle by the correct answer. Then answer the questions.

1. Beatrix Potter liked to _____ books.
   Ⓐ draw and write
   Ⓑ buy and sell
   Ⓒ copy and share

2. Potter liked to draw things from _____.
   Ⓐ stores
   Ⓑ books
   Ⓒ nature

3. What was the title of Potter's first book?

   _____

4. How many sisters does Peter Rabbit have? How do you know?

   _____

   _____

Write About the Topic

Use the Writing Form to draw and write about what you read.

Draw Peter and his sisters. Write about Beatrix Potter's life before and after she made the book.

A Famous Illustrator

Many books have illustrations, or pictures. People who make this kind of art are called illustrators. Beatrix Potter was the author and illustrator of many books. She liked to make stories about rabbits and other small animals.

Potter was born in England in 1866. Her family stayed in the country in Scotland in the summers. Potter liked to be in nature. She spent a lot of time drawing and painting. She liked to make pictures of the insects and other animals she saw outside.

Potter drew many animals and plants in *The Tale of Peter Rabbit.*

Peter Rabbit, his sisters, and his mother

In 1902, Potter published her first book. It was called *The Tale of Peter Rabbit.* The book was very popular. It was about a little boy rabbit and his family. Peter Rabbit had three sisters. Their names were Flopsy, Mopsy, and Cotton-tail. All of these characters are still popular today.

Nonfiction Reading Practice • EMC 3231 • © Evan-Moor Corp.

A Famous Illustrator

Fill in the circle by the correct answer. Then answer the questions.

1. People who draw pictures for books are called _____.
   - Ⓐ authors
   - Ⓑ illustrators
   - Ⓒ publishers

2. Beatrix Potter liked to draw things from _____.
   - Ⓐ nature
   - Ⓑ England
   - Ⓒ other books

3. What are two things Potter drew in *The Tale of Peter Rabbit?*

   _____

4. What other characters were in *The Tale of Peter Rabbit?*

   _____

   _____

Write About the Topic

Use the Writing Form to draw and write about what you read.

Draw one of Beatrix Potter's characters.
Write to tell about Beatrix Potter's life.

Community Art

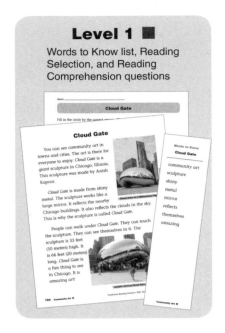

Level 1 ■
Words to Know list, Reading Selection, and Reading Comprehension questions

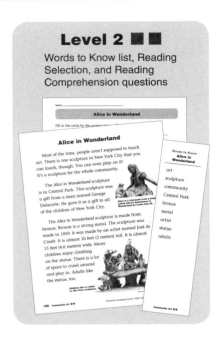

Level 2 ■ ■
Words to Know list, Reading Selection, and Reading Comprehension questions

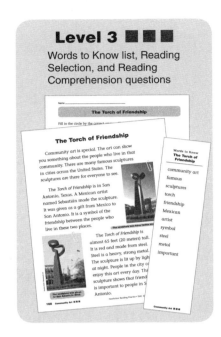

Level 3 ■ ■ ■
Words to Know list, Reading Selection, and Reading Comprehension questions

Assemble the Unit

Reproduce and distribute one copy for each student:

- Visual Literacy page: Kinds of Community Art, page 161
- Level 1, 2, or 3 Reading Selection and Reading Comprehension page and the corresponding Words to Know list
- Graphic Organizer of your choosing, provided on pages 180–186
- Writing Form: Community Art, page 162

Visual Literacy

Introduce the Topic

Review and discuss the different kinds of community art. Explain that community art belongs to the city or town where it is located. Ask students to describe public art that they have seen in person.

Read and Respond

Form leveled groups and review the Words to Know lists with each group of students. Instruct each group to read their selection individually, in pairs, or as a group. Have students complete the Reading Comprehension page for their selection.

Writing Form

Write About the Topic

Read aloud the leveled writing prompt for each group. Tell students to use the Graphic Organizer to plan their writing. Direct students to use their Writing Form to respond to their prompt.

Kinds of Community Art

Water fountain

J.C. Nichols Memorial Fountain
Kansas City, Missouri

Building

Los Angeles Public Library
Los Angeles, California

Mural painting

San Francisco, California

Statue
Statue of Abraham Lincoln
Washington, DC

Julien Hautcoeur / Shutterstock.com

Community Art

Words to Know	Words to Know	Words to Know
Cloud Gate	**Alice in Wonderland**	**The Torch of Friendship**
community art	art	community art
sculpture	sculpture	famous
shiny	community	sculptures
metal	Central Park	torch
mirror	bronze	friendship
reflects	metal	Mexican
themselves	artist	artist
amazing	statue	symbol
	adults	steel
		metal
		important

Cloud Gate

You can see community art in towns and cities. The art is there for everyone to enjoy. *Cloud Gate* is a giant sculpture in Chicago, Illinois. This sculpture was made by Anish Kapoor.

Cloud Gate is in Millennium Park

Cloud Gate is made from shiny metal. The sculpture works like a large mirror. It reflects the nearby Chicago buildings. It also reflects the clouds in the sky. This is why the sculpture is called *Cloud Gate*.

People can walk under *Cloud Gate*. They can touch the sculpture. They can see themselves in it. The sculpture is 33 feet (10 meters) high. It is 66 feet (20 meters) long. *Cloud Gate* is a fun thing to see in Chicago. It is amazing art!

people visiting Cloud Gate

Nonfiction Reading Practice • EMC 3231 • © Evan-Moor Corp.

Name _____

Cloud Gate

Fill in the circle by the correct answer. Then answer the questions.

1. Community art is for _____ in a town or a city.
   - Ⓐ only a few people
   - Ⓑ everyone
   - Ⓒ an artist

2. *Cloud Gate* is made from _____.
   - Ⓐ gates
   - Ⓑ shiny metal
   - Ⓒ clouds

3. Where can people go to see the *Cloud Gate* sculpture?

   _____

4. What kind of reflections can people see in *Cloud Gate*?

   _____

   _____

Write About the Topic

Use the Writing Form to draw and write about what you read.

Draw *Cloud Gate*. Write to tell three things about this community art sculpture.

Alice in Wonderland

Most of the time, people aren't supposed to touch art. There is one sculpture in New York City that you can touch, though. You can even play on it! It's a sculpture for the whole community.

The *Alice in Wonderland* sculpture is in Central Park. This sculpture was a gift from a man named George Delacorte. He gave it as a gift to all of the children of New York City.

Alice is a character from a book called *Alice's Adventures in Wonderland* by Lewis Carroll.

The *Alice in Wonderland* sculpture is made from bronze. Bronze is a strong metal. The sculpture was made in 1959. It was made by an artist named José de Creeft. It is almost 10 feet (3 meters) tall. It is almost 15 feet (4.6 meters) wide. Many children enjoy climbing on the statue. There is a lot of space to crawl around and play in. Adults like the statue, too.

Children like to climb on the Alice sculpture.

DW labs Incorporated / Shutterstock.com

Nonfiction Reading Practice • EMC 3231 • © Evan-Moor Corp.

Name _____

Alice in Wonderland

Fill in the circle by the correct answer. Then answer the questions.

1. The *Alice in Wonderland* sculpture was made by _____.
   - Ⓐ George Delacorte
   - Ⓑ Lewis Carroll
   - Ⓒ José de Creeft

2. The sculpture was a gift to _____ of New York City.
   - Ⓐ the children
   - Ⓑ the artists
   - Ⓒ one family

3. What does the *Alice in Wonderland* sculpture look like?

   _____

4. What is the main idea of the text?

   _____

   _____

Write About the Topic

Use the Writing Form to draw and write about what you read.

Draw one part of the Alice sculpture. Why is this sculpture special? Write to tell about it.

The Torch of Friendship

Community art is special. The art can show you something about the people who live in that community. There are many famous sculptures in cities across the United States. The sculptures are there for everyone to see.

The *Torch of Friendship* is in San Antonio, Texas. A Mexican artist named Sebastián made the sculpture. It was given as a gift from Mexico to San Antonio. It is a symbol of the friendship between the people who live in these two places.

The sculpture has many twists and turns.

The sculpture was given to San Antonio in 2002.

The *Torch of Friendship* is almost 65 feet (20 meters) tall. It is red and made from steel. Steel is a heavy, strong metal. The sculpture is lit up by lights at night. People in the city can enjoy this art every day. This sculpture shows that friendship is important to people in San Antonio.

Nonfiction Reading Practice • EMC 3231 • © Evan-Moor Corp.

Name _____

The Torch of Friendship

Fill in the circle by the correct answer. Then answer the questions.

1. The *Torch of Friendship* was given as a gift in _____.
   Ⓐ 2000
   Ⓑ 2001
   Ⓒ 2002

2. The *Torch of Friendship* is a _____.
   Ⓐ sculpture
   Ⓑ building
   Ⓒ painting

3. What is the *Torch of Friendship* made from?

   _____

4. What does the *Torch of Friendship* show you about people in San Antonio and Mexico?

   _____

   _____

Write About the Topic

Use the Writing Form to draw and write about what you read.

Draw the *Torch of Friendship*. Write to tell about it and where it came from.

Pottery

Level 1 ■
Words to Know list, Reading Selection, and Reading Comprehension questions

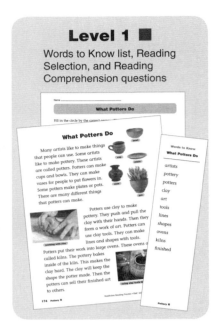

Level 2 ■ ■
Words to Know list, Reading Selection, and Reading Comprehension questions

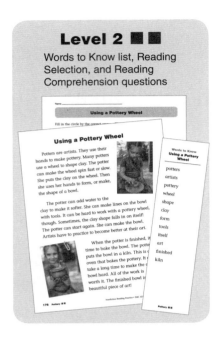

Level 3 ■ ■ ■
Words to Know list, Reading Selection, and Reading Comprehension questions

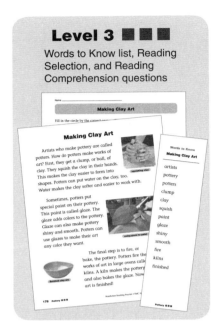

Assemble the Unit

Reproduce and distribute one copy for each student:

- Visual Literacy page: Pottery Supplies, page 171
- Level 1, 2, or 3 Reading Selection and Reading Comprehension page and the corresponding Words to Know list
- Graphic Organizer of your choosing, provided on pages 180–186
- Writing Form: Pottery, page 172

Visual Literacy

Introduce the Topic

Review the images and names of the pottery supplies. Explain that the kiln is electric and works much like a kitchen oven. Ask students to describe their personal experiences working with clay, such as in art class.

Read and Respond

Form leveled groups and review the Words to Know lists with each group of students. Instruct each group to read their selection individually, in pairs, or as a group. Have students complete the Reading Comprehension page for their selection.

Writing Form

Write About the Topic

Read aloud the leveled writing prompt for each group. Tell students to use the Graphic Organizer to plan their writing. Direct students to use their Writing Form to respond to their prompt.

Pottery Supplies

clay

pottery wheel

pottery kiln

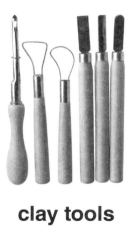

clay tools

pottery in a kiln

Name _____

Pottery

Words to Know

What Potters Do

artists
pottery
potters
clay
art
tools
lines
shapes
ovens
kilns
finished

Pottery ■

Words to Know

Using a Pottery Wheel

potters
artists
pottery
wheel
shape
clay
form
tools
itself
art
finished
kiln

Pottery ■■

Words to Know

Making Clay Art

artists
pottery
potters
clump
clay
squish
paint
glaze
shiny
smooth
fire
kilns
finished

Pottery ■■■

What Potters Do

bowl

cup

plate

vase

pot

Many artists like to make things that people can use. Some artists like to make pottery. These artists are called potters. Potters can make cups and bowls. They can make vases for people to put flowers in. Some potters make plates or pots. There are many different things that potters can make.

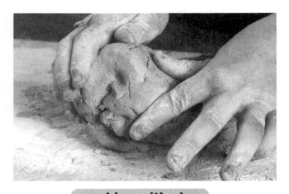

working with clay

Potters use clay to make pottery. They push and pull the clay with their hands. Then they form a work of art. Potters can use clay tools. They can make lines and shapes with tools.

Potters put their work into large ovens. These ovens are called kilns. The pottery bakes inside of the kiln. This makes the clay hard. The clay will keep the shape the potter made. Then the potters can sell their finished art to others.

using clay tools to make designs

What Potters Do

Fill in the circle by the correct answer. Then answer the questions.

1. Artists who make pottery are called _____.
    - Ⓐ vases
    - Ⓑ kilns
    - Ⓒ potters

2. Artists can use _____ to make lines and shapes on clay.
    - Ⓐ clay tools
    - Ⓑ kilns
    - Ⓒ cups

3. What is the main idea of the text?

    _____

4. Write the sentences that tell you what potters do to bake their clay art.

    _____

    _____

Write About the Topic

Use the Writing Form to draw and write about what you read.

Draw a clay cup. Write to tell how potters make their pottery.

Using a Pottery Wheel

Potters are artists. They use their hands to make pottery. Many potters use a wheel to shape clay. The potter can make the wheel spin fast or slow. She puts the clay on the wheel. Then she uses her hands to form, or make, the shape of a bowl.

The potter can add water to the clay to make it softer. She can make lines on the bowl with tools. It can be hard to work with a pottery wheel, though. Sometimes, the clay shape falls in on itself! The potter can start again. She can make the bowl. Artists have to practice to become better at their art.

When the potter is finished, it's time to bake the bowl. The potter puts the bowl in a kiln. This is an oven that bakes the pottery. It can take a long time to make the clay bowl hard. All of the work is worth it. The finished bowl is a beautiful piece of art!

Nonfiction Reading Practice • EMC 3231 • © Evan-Moor Corp.

Using a Pottery Wheel

Fill in the circle by the correct answer. Then answer the questions.

1. The potter uses a wheel to make a _____.
   Ⓐ ball of clay
   Ⓑ clay bowl
   Ⓒ pottery kiln

2. Potters need _____ to become good artists.
   Ⓐ luck
   Ⓑ water
   Ⓒ practice

3. Why can it be hard to use a pottery wheel?

   _____

4. Why does the potter bake the bowl?

   _____

   _____

Write About the Topic

Use the Writing Form to draw and write about what you read.

Draw a clay bowl on a wheel. Write to tell how potters use wheels to make works of art.

Making Clay Art

squishing clay

Artists who make pottery are called potters. How do potters make works of art? First, they get a clump, or ball, of clay. They squish the clay in their hands. This makes the clay easier to form into shapes. Potters can put water on the clay, too. Water makes the clay softer and easier to work with.

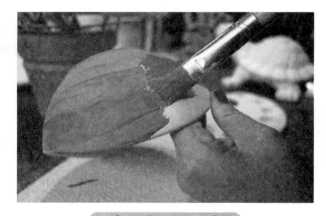

using glaze to paint

Sometimes, potters put special paint on their pottery. This paint is called glaze. The glaze adds colors to the pottery. Glaze can also make pottery shiny and smooth. Potters can use glazes to make their art any color they want.

finished clay art

The final step is to fire, or bake, the pottery. Potters fire their works of art in large ovens called kilns. A kiln makes the pottery hard and also bakes the glaze. Now the art is finished!

Nonfiction Reading Practice • EMC 3231 • © Evan-Moor Corp.

Making Clay Art

Fill in the circle by the correct answer. Then answer the questions.

1. Potters start to make pottery art with a _____.
   Ⓐ clump of clay
   Ⓑ bowl of paint
   Ⓒ hot kiln

2. Water helps potters _____ clay more easily.
   Ⓐ paint
   Ⓑ bake
   Ⓒ shape

3. How can potters add colors to their works of art?

   _____

4. Why is the kiln important in making pottery?

   _____

   _____

Write About the Topic

Use the Writing Form to draw and write about what you read.

Draw a piece of pottery art. Write to tell how potters make and color their art.

T-Chart

Famous Person

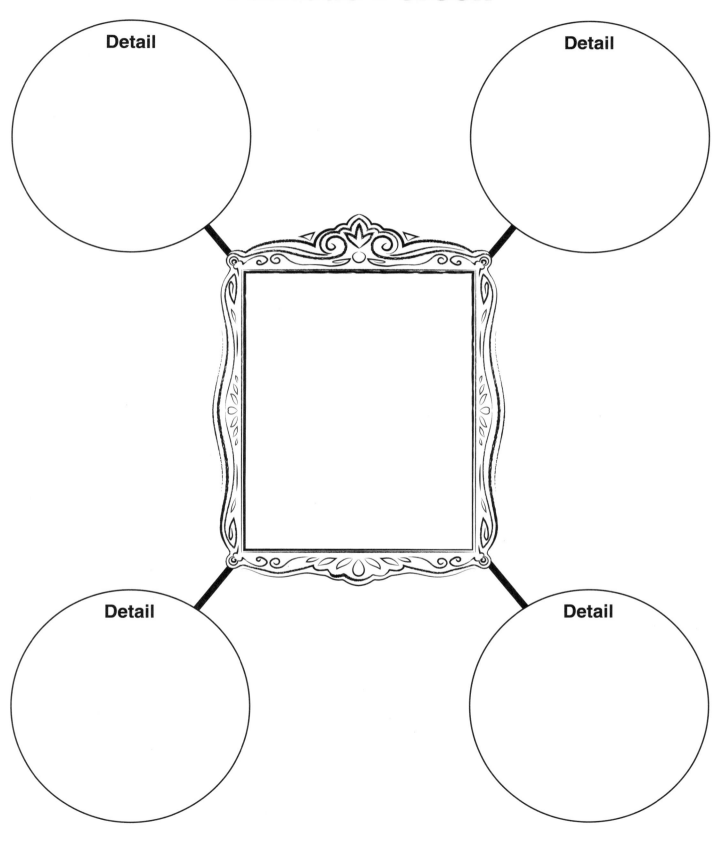

Detail

Detail

Detail

Detail

Name _____

Use Five Senses

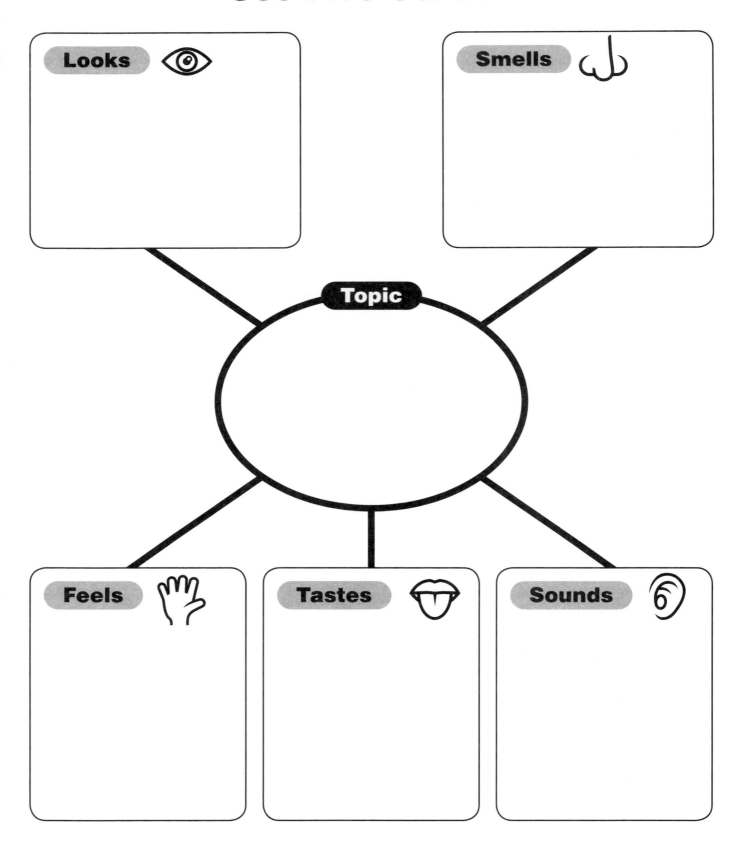

Looks 👁

Smells 👃

Topic

Feels ✋

Tastes 👅

Sounds 👂

Nonfiction Reading Practice • EMC 3231 • © Evan-Moor Corp.

Name _____

Tell It In Order

1 First

2 Next

3 Then

4 Last

Topic: _____

K	**What I Know**

W	**What I Want to Know**

L	**What I Learned**

Name

Same or Different?

Both

1.

2.

All About It

Topic

[ ]

Details

Who: _____

What: _____

When: _____

Where: _____

Why: _____

How: _____

Nonfiction Reading Practice • EMC 3231 • © Evan-Moor Corp.

Answer Key

Page 15

Name _____

Fly to the Moon

Fill in the circle by the correct answer. Then answer the questions.

1. Neil Armstrong was the first person to _____.
   - Ⓐ go around the moon
   - Ⓑ fly in a spaceship
   - ● walk on the moon

2. The three astronauts went to the moon in _____.
   - ● 1969
   - Ⓑ 1968
   - Ⓒ 1967

3. How did the astronauts help people learn more about the moon?

   <u>They took rocks and soil back to Earth.</u>

4. What was the main idea of the text?

   <u>Three astronauts were the first people to</u>

   <u>go to the moon. We learned from their visit.</u>

Write About the Topic
Use the Writing Form to draw and write about what you read.

Draw Neil Armstrong on the moon.
Write about one thing he did there.

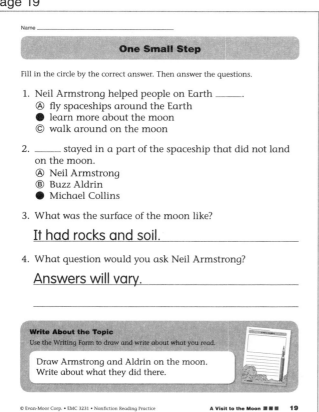

A Visit to the Moon ■ 15

Page 17

Name _____

Walk on the Moon

Fill in the circle by the correct answer. Then answer the questions.

1. Astronauts are people who _____.
   - Ⓐ study space on Earth
   - ● go to space
   - Ⓒ study soil and rocks

2. _____ said, "The Eagle has landed."
   - ● Neil Armstrong
   - Ⓑ Buzz Aldrin
   - Ⓒ Michael Collins

3. What can you learn about astronauts from the photos?

   <u>They wear special clothes.</u>

4. What did Armstrong and Aldrin do on the moon?

   <u>They studied the area around them. They</u>

   <u>took rocks and soil and put up a flag.</u>

Write About the Topic
Use the Writing Form to draw and write about what you read.

Draw one of the three astronauts. Write
about what that person did in space.

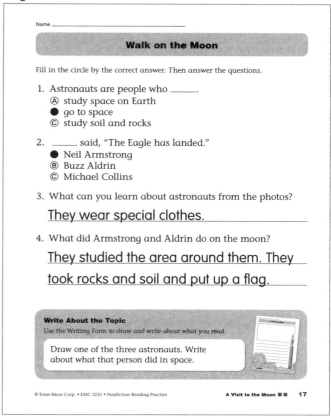

A Visit to the Moon ■ ■ 17

Page 19

Name _____

One Small Step

Fill in the circle by the correct answer. Then answer the questions.

1. Neil Armstrong helped people on Earth _____.
   - Ⓐ fly spaceships around the Earth
   - ● learn more about the moon
   - Ⓒ walk around on the moon

2. _____ stayed in a part of the spaceship that did not land on the moon.
   - Ⓐ Neil Armstrong
   - Ⓑ Buzz Aldrin
   - ● Michael Collins

3. What was the surface of the moon like?

   <u>It had rocks and soil.</u>

4. What question would you ask Neil Armstrong?

   <u>Answers will vary.</u>

Write About the Topic
Use the Writing Form to draw and write about what you read.

Draw Armstrong and Aldrin on the moon.
Write about what they did there.

A Visit to the Moon ■ ■ ■ 19

Page 25

Name _____

Life Long Ago

Fill in the circle by the correct answer. Then answer the questions.

1. History is what happened in the _____.
   - ● past
   - Ⓑ present
   - Ⓒ future

2. You can find objects from history in a _____.
   - Ⓐ timeline
   - Ⓑ new place
   - ● museum

3. What can looking at old objects help you learn?

   <u>How people lived in the past</u>

4. Tell about one object you can see at a museum.

   <u>You can see a cup that is 3,000 years old.</u>

Write About the Topic
Use the Writing Form to write about what you read.

What are two things you can do to learn more
about life long ago?

Learn About History ■ 25

Page 27

Name _____

Events from History

Fill in the circle by the correct answer. Then answer the questions.

1. History is about the _____.
   Ⓐ future
   Ⓑ present
   ● past

2. _____ things have happened in the past.
   Ⓐ Only good
   Ⓑ Only bad
   ● Both good and bad

3. Who is an important person in United States history?

   George Washington

4. Do people and places from the past look different from people and places today? Explain your answer.

   Yes, people are wearing different clothes.

   Their kitchens do not look like kitchens today.

Write About the Topic
Use the Writing Form to write about what you read.

Write three things you can do to learn more about an event from the past.

Page 29

Name _____

Life in the Past

Fill in the circle by the correct answer. Then answer the questions.

1. History is about what _____.
   Ⓐ is happening now
   ● has happened
   Ⓒ will happen

2. You can _____ to learn more about history.
   Ⓐ plan events
   ● read books
   Ⓒ make artifacts

3. What is an artifact?

   It is an object from the past.

4. What is one artifact you could see at a museum? Explain what it shows you about the past.

   Answers will vary. Example: A model of a house

   shows me that homes were different back then.

Write About the Topic
Use the Writing Form to write about what you read.

How can you learn more about people from the past?

Page 35

Name _____

Understand a Map

Fill in the circle by the correct answer. Then answer the questions.

1. A map is a _____ of a place.
   Ⓐ key
   Ⓑ symbol
   ● drawing

2. A map key has _____ that stand for different things.
   ● symbols
   Ⓑ directions
   Ⓒ trails

3. How are the four directions shown on a map?

   A symbol with the letters N, S, E, W

4. Imagine you are the person on the trail in Lake View Park. How can you get to the hills?

   Walk west on the trail. Then go south.

Write About the Topic
Use the Writing Form to draw and write about what you read.

Draw a new symbol to put on the Lake View Park map and key. Write to tell about your symbol.

Page 37

Name _____

Map Facts

Fill in the circle by the correct answer. Then answer the questions.

1. A map shows _____.
   Ⓐ when something will happen
   Ⓑ how something works
   ● how a place looks from above

2. A map _____ explains map symbols.
   ● key
   Ⓑ title
   Ⓒ direction

3. What is the symbol for the food area at the Town Carnival?

   A food stand; a hot dog cart

4. What do the letters N, S, E, and W stand for?

   north, south, east, west

Write About the Topic
Use the Writing Form to draw and write about what you read.

Draw your own compass rose. Write why a compass rose is important on a map.

Name _____

Using Maps

Fill in the circle by the correct answer. Then answer the questions.

1. A map key has _____ that stand for things.
   Ⓐ directions
   ● symbols
   Ⓒ titles

2. A _____ is a special symbol that shows directions.
   Ⓐ map key
   ● compass rose
   Ⓒ drawing of a place

3. What is west of the swimming pool in Greenville Square?

   <u>An art museum</u>

4. What can you use to help you understand a map?

   <u>The map title, map key, and compass rose</u>

Write About the Topic
Use the Writing Form to draw and write about what you read.

Draw a simple map of your classroom. Write directions to tell how to get from the teacher's desk to the door.

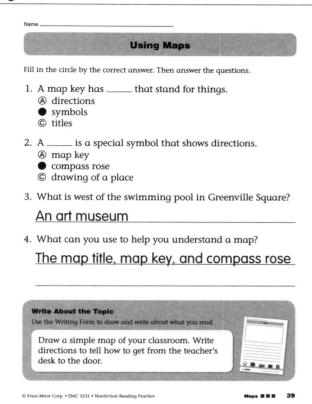

Name _____

Mid-Fall Festival

Fill in the circle by the correct answer. Then answer the questions.

1. A special food for the Mid-Fall Festival is _____.
   Ⓐ vegetables
   Ⓑ rice
   ● mooncakes

2. You can see a fire dragon in the Mid-Fall Festival _____.
   ● parade
   Ⓑ field
   Ⓒ yard

3. What is another name for the Mid-Fall Festival?

   <u>The Moon Festival</u>

4. How do people prepare for the Mid-Fall Festival?

   <u>They make mooncakes. They make big meals. They get ready for a parade.</u>

Write About the Topic
Use the Writing Form to draw and write about what you read.

Draw one thing from the Mid-Fall Festival. Write to tell how people celebrate the harvest.

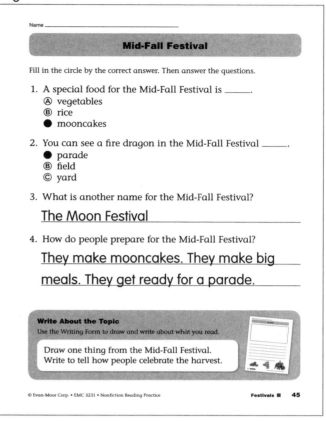

Name _____

Tulip Time Festival

Fill in the circle by the correct answer. Then answer the questions.

1. When do tulips bloom in Holland, Michigan?
   ● in the middle of May
   Ⓑ at the end of May
   Ⓒ at the beginning of May

2. The festival celebrates _____.
   Ⓐ shoes
   Ⓑ dancing
   ● Dutch ways

3. What did you learn about the Netherlands?

   <u>It is known for tulip flowers and windmills.</u>

4. Tell how the Tulip Time Festival celebrates the Dutch.

   <u>People at the festival eat Dutch food and wear Dutch clothes and shoes.</u>

Write About the Topic
Use the Writing Form to draw and write about what you read.

Draw two things you can see at the Tulip Time Festival. Write to tell about what happens there.

Name _____

The Holi Festival

Fill in the circle by the correct answer. Then answer the questions.

1. Holi is a festival where people toss _____.
   Ⓐ rice
   Ⓑ flowers
   ● powders

2. What do you think the word **wise** means in the text?
   ● smart
   Ⓑ sad
   Ⓒ poor

3. Why is Holi also called the Festival of Colors?

   <u>People get covered in colors.</u>

4. What do people do to show they are happy that good won over evil?

   <u>They light bonfires. They dance and sing.</u>

Write About the Topic
Use the Writing Form to draw and write about what you read.

Draw a person who is at the Festival of Colors. Write to tell what is happening.

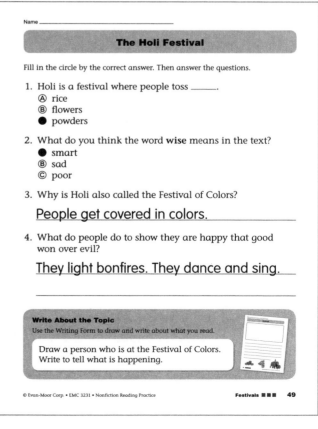

Page 55

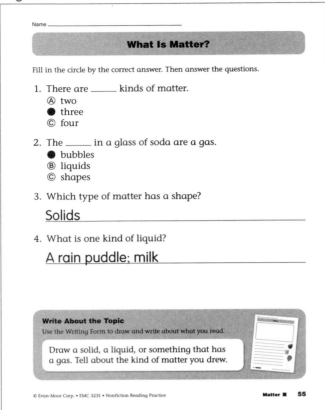

Name _____

What Is Matter?

Fill in the circle by the correct answer. Then answer the questions.

1. There are _____ kinds of matter.
   Ⓐ two
   ● three
   © four

2. The _____ in a glass of soda are a gas.
   ● bubbles
   Ⓑ liquids
   © shapes

3. Which type of matter has a shape?

   Solids

4. What is one kind of liquid?

   A rain puddle; milk

Write About the Topic
Use the Writing Form to draw and write about what you read.

Draw a solid, a liquid, or something that has a gas. Tell about the kind of matter you drew.

© Evan-Moor Corp. • EMC 3231 • Nonfiction Reading Practice   Matter ■   55

Page 57

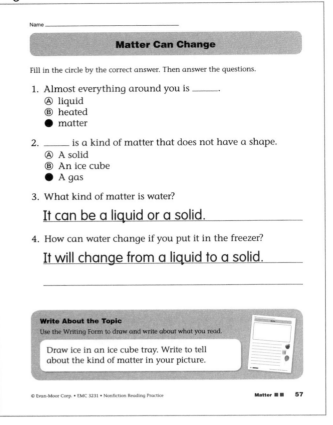

Name _____

Matter Can Change

Fill in the circle by the correct answer. Then answer the questions.

1. Almost everything around you is _____.
   Ⓐ liquid
   Ⓑ heated
   ● matter

2. _____ is a kind of matter that does not have a shape.
   Ⓐ A solid
   Ⓑ An ice cube
   ● A gas

3. What kind of matter is water?

   It can be a liquid or a solid.

4. How can water change if you put it in the freezer?

   It will change from a liquid to a solid.

Write About the Topic
Use the Writing Form to draw and write about what you read.

Draw ice in an ice cube tray. Write to tell about the kind of matter in your picture.

© Evan-Moor Corp. • EMC 3231 • Nonfiction Reading Practice   Matter ■ ■   57

Page 59

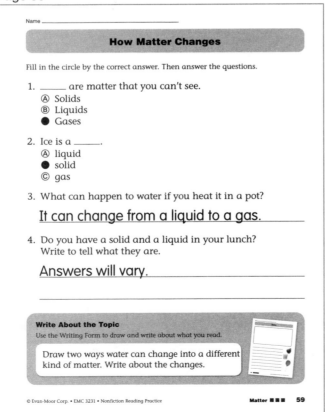

Name _____

How Matter Changes

Fill in the circle by the correct answer. Then answer the questions.

1. _____ are matter that you can't see.
   Ⓐ Solids
   Ⓑ Liquids
   ● Gases

2. Ice is a _____.
   Ⓐ liquid
   ● solid
   © gas

3. What can happen to water if you heat it in a pot?

   It can change from a liquid to a gas.

4. Do you have a solid and a liquid in your lunch?
   Write to tell what they are.

   Answers will vary.

Write About the Topic
Use the Writing Form to draw and write about what you read.

Draw two ways water can change into a different kind of matter. Write about the changes.

© Evan-Moor Corp. • EMC 3231 • Nonfiction Reading Practice   Matter ■ ■ ■   59

Page 65

Name _____

Habitats Are Homes

Fill in the circle by the correct answer. Then answer the questions.

1. A habitat is _____.
   Ⓐ an animal
   ● a home
   © a berry

2. A shelter is a place where an animal can _____.
   Ⓐ swim in water
   Ⓑ find berries
   ● live safely

3. What does the brown bear use for shelter?

   A cave

4. What do you know about the brown bear's habitat?

   The brown bear lives in a forest. It eats berries

   and drinks water. Its shelter is a cave.

Write About the Topic
Use the Writing Form to draw and write about what you read.

Draw and write about the things a brown bear needs to live.

© Evan-Moor Corp. • EMC 3231 • Nonfiction Reading Practice   Animal Habitats ■   65

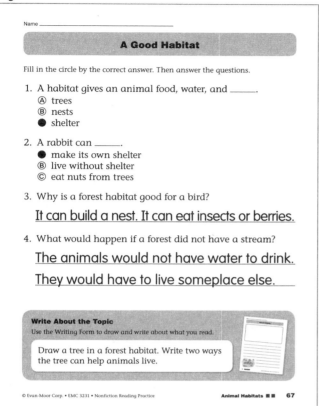

Name _____

A Good Habitat

Fill in the circle by the correct answer. Then answer the questions.

1. A habitat gives an animal food, water, and _____.
   Ⓐ trees
   Ⓑ nests
   ● shelter

2. A rabbit can _____.
   ● make its own shelter
   Ⓑ live without shelter
   Ⓒ eat nuts from trees

3. Why is a forest habitat good for a bird?

   It can build a nest. It can eat insects or berries.

4. What would happen if a forest did not have a stream?

   The animals would not have water to drink.
   They would have to live someplace else.

Write About the Topic
Use the Writing Form to draw and write about what you read.

Draw a tree in a forest habitat. Write two ways the tree can help animals live.

© Evan-Moor Corp. • EMC 3231 • Nonfiction Reading Practice   **Animal Habitats** ▣ ▣   67

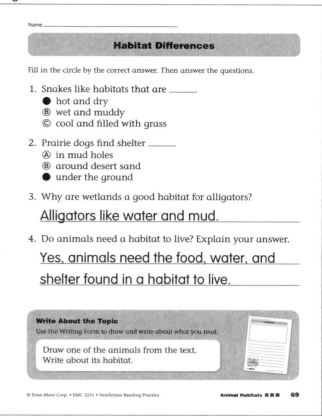

Name _____

Habitat Differences

Fill in the circle by the correct answer. Then answer the questions.

1. Snakes like habitats that are _____.
   ● hot and dry
   Ⓑ wet and muddy
   Ⓒ cool and filled with grass

2. Prairie dogs find shelter _____.
   Ⓐ in mud holes
   Ⓑ around desert sand
   ● under the ground

3. Why are wetlands a good habitat for alligators?

   Alligators like water and mud.

4. Do animals need a habitat to live? Explain your answer.

   Yes, animals need the food, water, and
   shelter found in a habitat to live.

Write About the Topic
Use the Writing Form to draw and write about what you read.

Draw one of the animals from the text. Write about its habitat.

© Evan-Moor Corp. • EMC 3231 • Nonfiction Reading Practice   **Animal Habitats** ▣ ▣ ▣   69

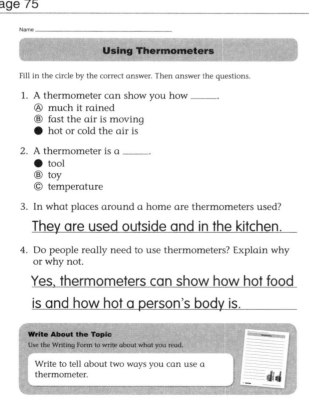

Name _____

Using Thermometers

Fill in the circle by the correct answer. Then answer the questions.

1. A thermometer can show you how _____.
   Ⓐ much it rained
   Ⓑ fast the air is moving
   ● hot or cold the air is

2. A thermometer is a _____.
   ● tool
   Ⓑ toy
   Ⓒ temperature

3. In what places around a home are thermometers used?

   They are used outside and in the kitchen.

4. Do people really need to use thermometers? Explain why or why not.

   Yes, thermometers can show how hot food
   is and how hot a person's body is.

Write About the Topic
Use the Writing Form to write about what you read.

Write to tell about two ways you can use a thermometer.

© Evan-Moor Corp. • EMC 3231 • Nonfiction Reading Practice   **Thermometers** ▣   75

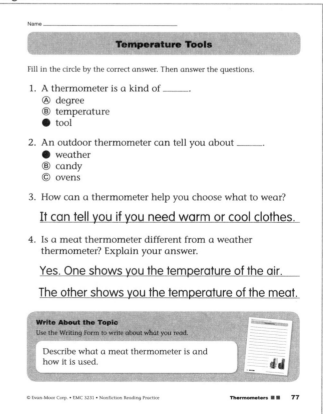

Name _____

Temperature Tools

Fill in the circle by the correct answer. Then answer the questions.

1. A thermometer is a kind of _____.
   Ⓐ degree
   Ⓑ temperature
   ● tool

2. An outdoor thermometer can tell you about _____.
   ● weather
   Ⓑ candy
   Ⓒ ovens

3. How can a thermometer help you choose what to wear?

   It can tell you if you need warm or cool clothes.

4. Is a meat thermometer different from a weather thermometer? Explain your answer.

   Yes. One shows you the temperature of the air.
   The other shows you the temperature of the meat.

Write About the Topic
Use the Writing Form to write about what you read.

Describe what a meat thermometer is and how it is used.

© Evan-Moor Corp. • EMC 3231 • Nonfiction Reading Practice   **Thermometers** ▣ ▣   77

Page 79

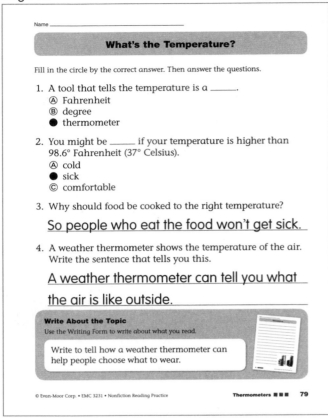

Name _____

What's the Temperature?

Fill in the circle by the correct answer. Then answer the questions.

1. A tool that tells the temperature is a _____.
   Ⓐ Fahrenheit
   Ⓑ degree
   ● thermometer

2. You might be _____ if your temperature is higher than 98.6° Fahrenheit (37° Celsius).
   Ⓐ cold
   ● sick
   Ⓒ comfortable

3. Why should food be cooked to the right temperature?

   So people who eat the food won't get sick.

4. A weather thermometer shows the temperature of the air. Write the sentence that tells you this.

   A weather thermometer can tell you what
   the air is like outside.

Write About the Topic
Use the Writing Form to write about what you read.

Write to tell how a weather thermometer can help people choose what to wear.

Page 85

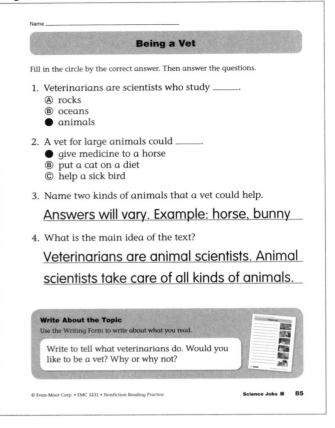

Name _____

Being a Vet

Fill in the circle by the correct answer. Then answer the questions.

1. Veterinarians are scientists who study _____.
   Ⓐ rocks
   Ⓑ oceans
   ● animals

2. A vet for large animals could _____.
   ● give medicine to a horse
   Ⓑ put a cat on a diet
   Ⓒ help a sick bird

3. Name two kinds of animals that a vet could help.

   Answers will vary. Example: horse, bunny

4. What is the main idea of the text?

   Veterinarians are animal scientists. Animal
   scientists take care of all kinds of animals.

Write About the Topic
Use the Writing Form to write about what you read.

Write to tell what veterinarians do. Would you like to be a vet? Why or why not?

Page 87

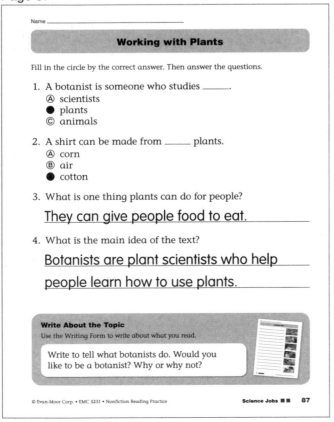

Name _____

Working with Plants

Fill in the circle by the correct answer. Then answer the questions.

1. A botanist is someone who studies _____.
   Ⓐ scientists
   ● plants
   Ⓒ animals

2. A shirt can be made from _____ plants.
   Ⓐ corn
   Ⓑ air
   ● cotton

3. What is one thing plants can do for people?

   They can give people food to eat.

4. What is the main idea of the text?

   Botanists are plant scientists who help
   people learn how to use plants.

Write About the Topic
Use the Writing Form to write about what you read.

Write to tell what botanists do. Would you like to be a botanist? Why or why not?

Page 89

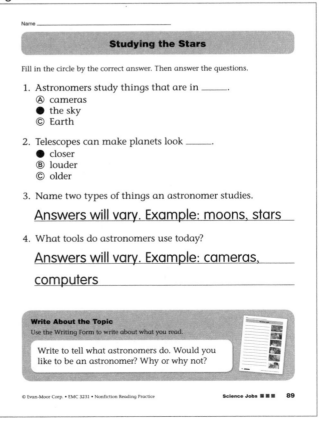

Name _____

Studying the Stars

Fill in the circle by the correct answer. Then answer the questions.

1. Astronomers study things that are in _____.
   Ⓐ cameras
   ● the sky
   Ⓒ Earth

2. Telescopes can make planets look _____.
   ● closer
   Ⓑ louder
   Ⓒ older

3. Name two types of things an astronomer studies.

   Answers will vary. Example: moons, stars

4. What tools do astronomers use today?

   Answers will vary. Example: cameras,
   computers

Write About the Topic
Use the Writing Form to write about what you read.

Write to tell what astronomers do. Would you like to be an astronomer? Why or why not?

Page 95

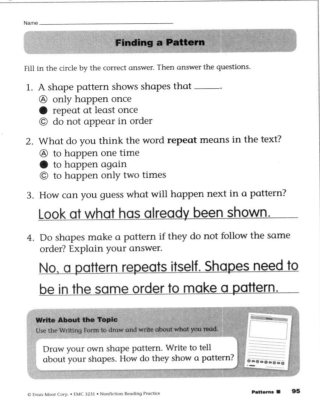

Name _____

Finding a Pattern

Fill in the circle by the correct answer. Then answer the questions.

1. A shape pattern shows shapes that _____.
   - Ⓐ only happen once
   - ● repeat at least once
   - Ⓒ do not appear in order

2. What do you think the word **repeat** means in the text?
   - Ⓐ to happen one time
   - ● to happen again
   - Ⓒ to happen only two times

3. How can you guess what will happen next in a pattern?

   Look at what has already been shown.

4. Do shapes make a pattern if they do not follow the same order? Explain your answer.

   No, a pattern repeats itself. Shapes need to be in the same order to make a pattern.

Write About the Topic
Use the Writing Form to draw and write about what you read.

Draw your own shape pattern. Write to tell about your shapes. How do they show a pattern?

© Evan-Moor Corp. • EMC 3231 • Nonfiction Reading Practice   Patterns ■   95

Page 97

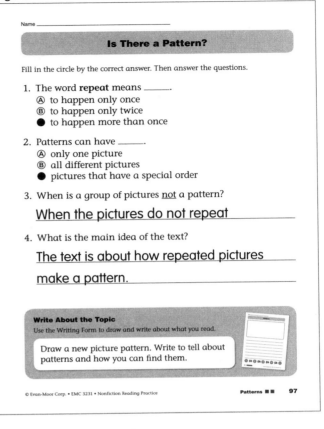

Name _____

Is There a Pattern?

Fill in the circle by the correct answer. Then answer the questions.

1. The word **repeat** means _____.
   - Ⓐ to happen only once
   - Ⓑ to happen only twice
   - ● to happen more than once

2. Patterns can have _____.
   - Ⓐ only one picture
   - Ⓑ all different pictures
   - ● pictures that have a special order

3. When is a group of pictures <u>not</u> a pattern?

   When the pictures do not repeat

4. What is the main idea of the text?

   The text is about how repeated pictures make a pattern.

Write About the Topic
Use the Writing Form to draw and write about what you read.

Draw a new picture pattern. Write to tell about patterns and how you can find them.

© Evan-Moor Corp. • EMC 3231 • Nonfiction Reading Practice   Patterns ■ ■   97

Page 99

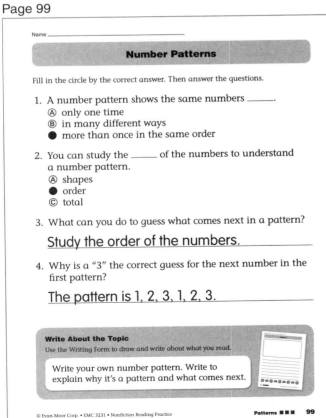

Name _____

Number Patterns

Fill in the circle by the correct answer. Then answer the questions.

1. A number pattern shows the same numbers _____.
   - Ⓐ only one time
   - Ⓑ in many different ways
   - ● more than once in the same order

2. You can study the _____ of the numbers to understand a number pattern.
   - Ⓐ shapes
   - ● order
   - Ⓒ total

3. What can you do to guess what comes next in a pattern?

   Study the order of the numbers.

4. Why is a "3" the correct guess for the next number in the first pattern?

   The pattern is 1, 2, 3, 1, 2, 3.

Write About the Topic
Use the Writing Form to draw and write about what you read.

Write your own number pattern. Write to explain why it's a pattern and what comes next.

© Evan-Moor Corp. • EMC 3231 • Nonfiction Reading Practice   Patterns ■ ■ ■   99

Page 105

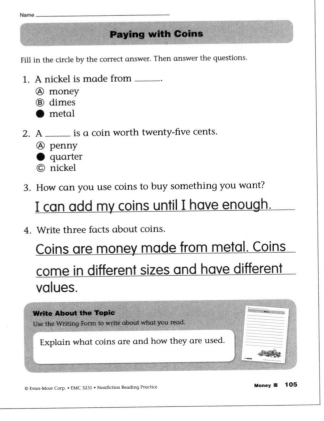

Name _____

Paying with Coins

Fill in the circle by the correct answer. Then answer the questions.

1. A nickel is made from _____.
   - Ⓐ money
   - Ⓑ dimes
   - ● metal

2. A _____ is a coin worth twenty-five cents.
   - Ⓐ penny
   - ● quarter
   - Ⓒ nickel

3. How can you use coins to buy something you want?

   I can add my coins until I have enough.

4. Write three facts about coins.

   Coins are money made from metal. Coins come in different sizes and have different values.

Write About the Topic
Use the Writing Form to write about what you read.

Explain what coins are and how they are used.

© Evan-Moor Corp. • EMC 3231 • Nonfiction Reading Practice   Money ■   105

Page 107

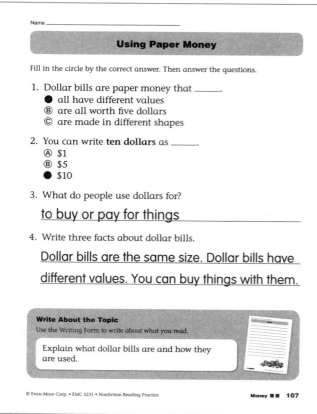

Name _____

Using Paper Money

Fill in the circle by the correct answer. Then answer the questions.

1. Dollar bills are paper money that _____.
   ● all have different values
   Ⓑ are all worth five dollars
   Ⓒ are made in different shapes

2. You can write **ten dollars** as _____.
   Ⓐ $1
   Ⓑ $5
   ● $10

3. What do people use dollars for?

   to buy or pay for things

4. Write three facts about dollar bills.

   Dollar bills are the same size. Dollar bills have

   different values. You can buy things with them.

Write About the Topic
Use the Writing Form to write about what you read.

Explain what dollar bills are and how they are used.

© Evan-Moor Corp. • EMC 3231 • Nonfiction Reading Practice   Money ■■ 107

Page 109

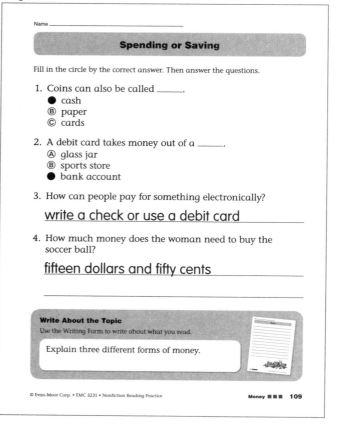

Name _____

Spending or Saving

Fill in the circle by the correct answer. Then answer the questions.

1. Coins can also be called _____.
   ● cash
   Ⓑ paper
   Ⓒ cards

2. A debit card takes money out of a _____.
   Ⓐ glass jar
   Ⓑ sports store
   ● bank account

3. How can people pay for something electronically?

   write a check or use a debit card

4. How much money does the woman need to buy the soccer ball?

   fifteen dollars and fifty cents

Write About the Topic
Use the Writing Form to write about what you read.

Explain three different forms of money.

© Evan-Moor Corp. • EMC 3231 • Nonfiction Reading Practice   Money ■■■ 109

Page 115

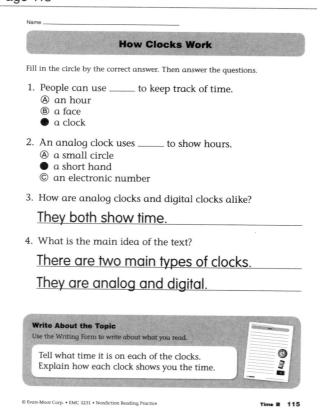

Name _____

How Clocks Work

Fill in the circle by the correct answer. Then answer the questions.

1. People can use _____ to keep track of time.
   Ⓐ an hour
   Ⓑ a face
   ● a clock

2. An analog clock uses _____ to show hours.
   Ⓐ a small circle
   ● a short hand
   Ⓒ an electronic number

3. How are analog clocks and digital clocks alike?

   They both show time.

4. What is the main idea of the text?

   There are two main types of clocks.

   They are analog and digital.

Write About the Topic
Use the Writing Form to write about what you read.

Tell what time it is on each of the clocks. Explain how each clock shows you the time.

© Evan-Moor Corp. • EMC 3231 • Nonfiction Reading Practice   Time ■ 115

Page 117

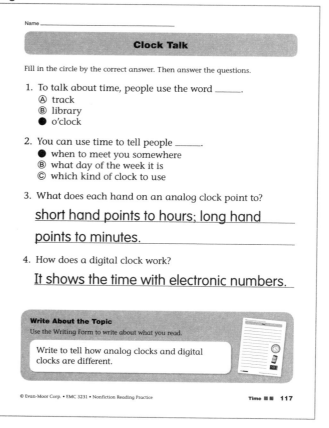

Name _____

Clock Talk

Fill in the circle by the correct answer. Then answer the questions.

1. To talk about time, people use the word _____.
   Ⓐ track
   Ⓑ library
   ● o'clock

2. You can use time to tell people _____.
   ● when to meet you somewhere
   Ⓑ what day of the week it is
   Ⓒ which kind of clock to use

3. What does each hand on an analog clock point to?

   short hand points to hours; long hand

   points to minutes.

4. How does a digital clock work?

   It shows the time with electronic numbers.

Write About the Topic
Use the Writing Form to write about what you read.

Write to tell how analog clocks and digital clocks are different.

© Evan-Moor Corp. • EMC 3231 • Nonfiction Reading Practice   Time ■■ 117

Page 119

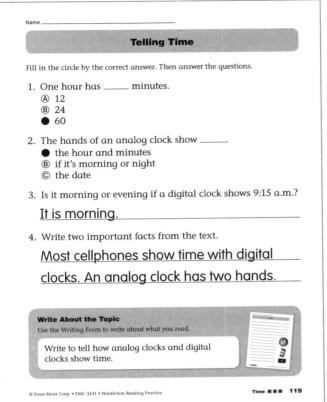

Name _____

Telling Time

Fill in the circle by the correct answer. Then answer the questions.

1. One hour has _____ minutes.
   - Ⓐ 12
   - Ⓑ 24
   - ● 60

2. The hands of an analog clock show _____.
   - ● the hour and minutes
   - Ⓑ if it's morning or night
   - Ⓒ the date

3. Is it morning or evening if a digital clock shows 9:15 a.m.?

   It is morning.

4. Write two important facts from the text.

   Most cellphones show time with digital
   clocks. An analog clock has two hands.

Write About the Topic
Use the Writing Form to write about what you read.

Write to tell how analog clocks and digital clocks show time.

© Evan-Moor Corp. • EMC 3231 • Nonfiction Reading Practice

Time ■■■ 119

Page 125

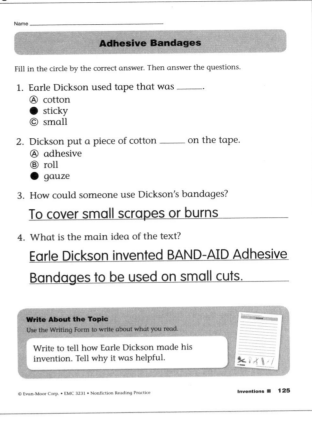

Name _____

Adhesive Bandages

Fill in the circle by the correct answer. Then answer the questions.

1. Earle Dickson used tape that was _____.
   - Ⓐ cotton
   - ● sticky
   - Ⓒ small

2. Dickson put a piece of cotton _____ on the tape.
   - Ⓐ adhesive
   - Ⓑ roll
   - ● gauze

3. How could someone use Dickson's bandages?

   To cover small scrapes or burns

4. What is the main idea of the text?

   Earle Dickson invented BAND-AID Adhesive
   Bandages to be used on small cuts.

Write About the Topic
Use the Writing Form to write about what you read.

Write to tell how Earle Dickson made his invention. Tell why it was helpful.

© Evan-Moor Corp. • EMC 3231 • Nonfiction Reading Practice

Inventions ■ 125

Page 127

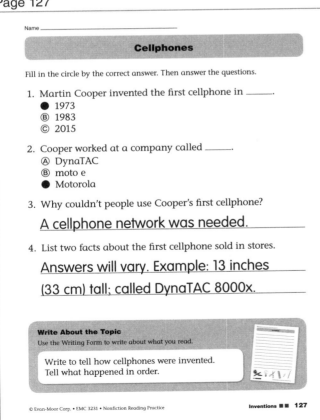

Name _____

Cellphones

Fill in the circle by the correct answer. Then answer the questions.

1. Martin Cooper invented the first cellphone in _____.
   - ● 1973
   - Ⓑ 1983
   - Ⓒ 2015

2. Cooper worked at a company called _____.
   - Ⓐ DynaTAC
   - Ⓑ moto e
   - ● Motorola

3. Why couldn't people use Cooper's first cellphone?

   A cellphone network was needed.

4. List two facts about the first cellphone sold in stores.

   Answers will vary. Example: 13 inches
   (33 cm) tall; called DynaTAC 8000x.

Write About the Topic
Use the Writing Form to write about what you read.

Write to tell how cellphones were invented. Tell what happened in order.

© Evan-Moor Corp. • EMC 3231 • Nonfiction Reading Practice

Inventions ■■ 127

Page 129

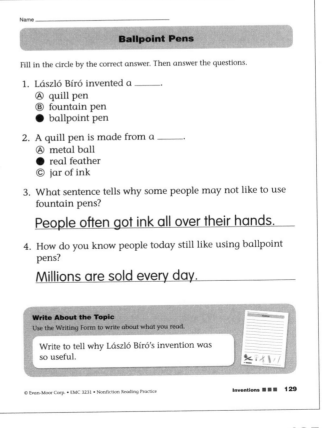

Name _____

Ballpoint Pens

Fill in the circle by the correct answer. Then answer the questions.

1. László Bíró invented a _____.
   - Ⓐ quill pen
   - Ⓑ fountain pen
   - ● ballpoint pen

2. A quill pen is made from a _____.
   - Ⓐ metal ball
   - ● real feather
   - Ⓒ jar of ink

3. What sentence tells why some people may not like to use fountain pens?

   People often got ink all over their hands.

4. How do you know people today still like using ballpoint pens?

   Millions are sold every day.

Write About the Topic
Use the Writing Form to write about what you read.

Write to tell why László Bíró's invention was so useful.

© Evan-Moor Corp. • EMC 3231 • Nonfiction Reading Practice

Inventions ■■■ 129

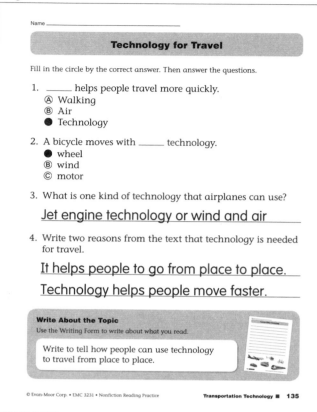

Name _____

Technology for Travel

Fill in the circle by the correct answer. Then answer the questions.

1. _____ helps people travel more quickly.
   Ⓐ Walking
   Ⓑ Air
   ● Technology

2. A bicycle moves with _____ technology.
   ● wheel
   Ⓑ wind
   Ⓒ motor

3. What is one kind of technology that airplanes can use?

   <u>Jet engine technology or wind and air</u>

4. Write two reasons from the text that technology is needed for travel.

   <u>It helps people to go from place to place.</u>

   <u>Technology helps people move faster.</u>

Write About the Topic
Use the Writing Form to write about what you read.

Write to tell how people can use technology to travel from place to place.

© Evan-Moor Corp. • EMC 3231 • Nonfiction Reading Practice   **Transportation Technology** ■ **135**

Name _____

Bicycles and Cars

Fill in the circle by the correct answer. Then answer the questions.

1. A person uses his or her _____ to make a bicycle move.
   Ⓐ hands
   Ⓑ keys
   ● feet

2. Most cars use _____ to get power.
   ● gasoline
   Ⓑ wheels
   Ⓒ people

3. What kind of technology do cars use?

   <u>Motor technology</u>

4. Are pedals an important part of bicycle and car technology? Explain why or why not.

   <u>Yes, bicycle pedals move the wheels and</u>

   <u>car pedals make the car motor stop or go.</u>

Write About the Topic
Use the Writing Form to write about what you read.

Write to tell about bicycle and car technologies. Tell how they are alike and different.

© Evan-Moor Corp. • EMC 3231 • Nonfiction Reading Practice   **Transportation Technology** ■ ■ **137**

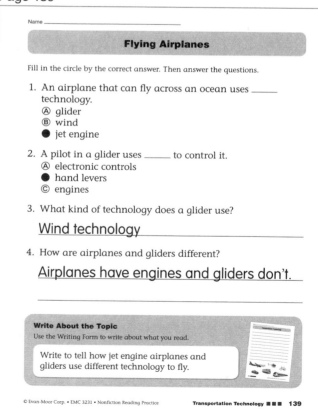

Name _____

Flying Airplanes

Fill in the circle by the correct answer. Then answer the questions.

1. An airplane that can fly across an ocean uses _____ technology.
   Ⓐ glider
   Ⓑ wind
   ● jet engine

2. A pilot in a glider uses _____ to control it.
   Ⓐ electronic controls
   ● hand levers
   Ⓒ engines

3. What kind of technology does a glider use?

   <u>Wind technology</u>

4. How are airplanes and gliders different?

   <u>Airplanes have engines and gliders don't.</u>

Write About the Topic
Use the Writing Form to write about what you read.

Write to tell how jet engine airplanes and gliders use different technology to fly.

© Evan-Moor Corp. • EMC 3231 • Nonfiction Reading Practice   **Transportation Technology** ■ ■ ■ **139**

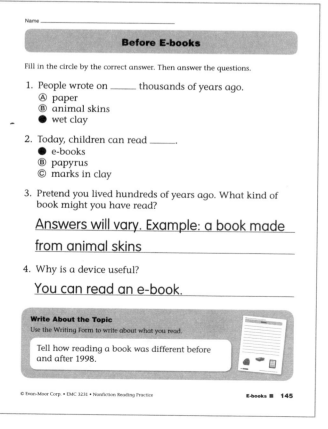

Name _____

Before E-books

Fill in the circle by the correct answer. Then answer the questions.

1. People wrote on _____ thousands of years ago.
   Ⓐ paper
   Ⓑ animal skins
   ● wet clay

2. Today, children can read _____.
   ● e-books
   Ⓑ papyrus
   Ⓒ marks in clay

3. Pretend you lived hundreds of years ago. What kind of book might you have read?

   <u>Answers will vary. Example: a book made</u>

   <u>from animal skins</u>

4. Why is a device useful?

   <u>You can read an e-book.</u>

Write About the Topic
Use the Writing Form to write about what you read.

Tell how reading a book was different before and after 1998.

© Evan-Moor Corp. • EMC 3231 • Nonfiction Reading Practice   **E-books** ■ **145**

Page 147

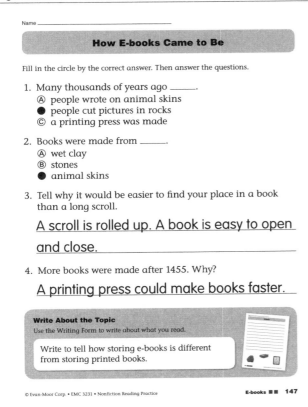

Name _____

How E-books Came to Be

Fill in the circle by the correct answer. Then answer the questions.

1. Many thousands of years ago _____.
   - Ⓐ people wrote on animal skins
   - ● people cut pictures in rocks
   - Ⓒ a printing press was made

2. Books were made from _____.
   - Ⓐ wet clay
   - Ⓑ stones
   - ● animal skins

3. Tell why it would be easier to find your place in a book than a long scroll.

   <u>A scroll is rolled up. A book is easy to open and close.</u>

4. More books were made after 1455. Why?

   <u>A printing press could make books faster.</u>

Write About the Topic
Use the Writing Form to write about what you read.

Write to tell how storing e-books is different from storing printed books.

E-books ■■ 147

Page 149

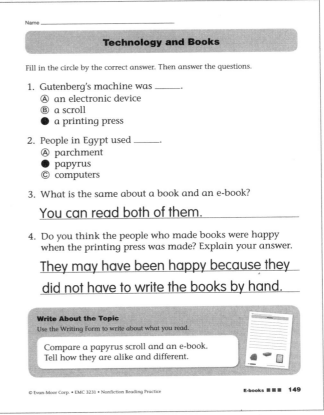

Name _____

Technology and Books

Fill in the circle by the correct answer. Then answer the questions.

1. Gutenberg's machine was _____.
   - Ⓐ an electronic device
   - Ⓑ a scroll
   - ● a printing press

2. People in Egypt used _____.
   - Ⓐ parchment
   - ● papyrus
   - Ⓒ computers

3. What is the same about a book and an e-book?

   <u>You can read both of them.</u>

4. Do you think the people who made books were happy when the printing press was made? Explain your answer.

   <u>They may have been happy because they did not have to write the books by hand.</u>

Write About the Topic
Use the Writing Form to write about what you read.

Compare a papyrus scroll and an e-book. Tell how they are alike and different.

E-books ■■■ 149

Page 155

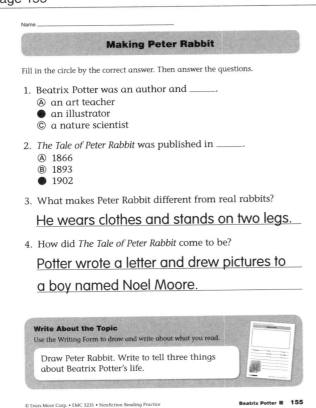

Name _____

Making Peter Rabbit

Fill in the circle by the correct answer. Then answer the questions.

1. Beatrix Potter was an author and _____.
   - Ⓐ an art teacher
   - ● an illustrator
   - Ⓒ a nature scientist

2. *The Tale of Peter Rabbit* was published in _____.
   - Ⓐ 1866
   - Ⓑ 1893
   - ● 1902

3. What makes Peter Rabbit different from real rabbits?

   <u>He wears clothes and stands on two legs.</u>

4. How did *The Tale of Peter Rabbit* come to be?

   <u>Potter wrote a letter and drew pictures to a boy named Noel Moore.</u>

Write About the Topic
Use the Writing Form to draw and write about what you read.

Draw Peter Rabbit. Write to tell three things about Beatrix Potter's life.

Beatrix Potter ■ 155

Page 157

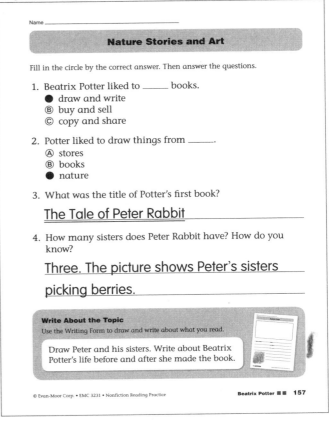

Name _____

Nature Stories and Art

Fill in the circle by the correct answer. Then answer the questions.

1. Beatrix Potter liked to _____ books.
   - ● draw and write
   - Ⓑ buy and sell
   - Ⓒ copy and share

2. Potter liked to draw things from _____.
   - Ⓐ stores
   - Ⓑ books
   - ● nature

3. What was the title of Potter's first book?

   <u>The Tale of Peter Rabbit</u>

4. How many sisters does Peter Rabbit have? How do you know?

   <u>Three. The picture shows Peter's sisters picking berries.</u>

Write About the Topic
Use the Writing Form to draw and write about what you read.

Draw Peter and his sisters. Write about Beatrix Potter's life before and after she made the book.

Beatrix Potter ■■ 157

Page 159

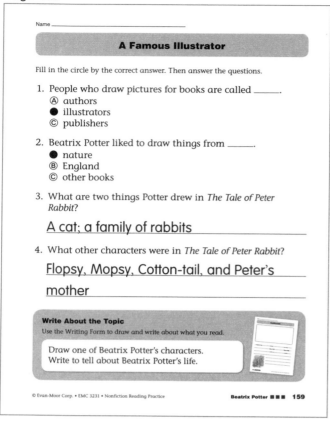

Name _____

A Famous Illustrator

Fill in the circle by the correct answer. Then answer the questions.

1. People who draw pictures for books are called _____.
   - Ⓐ authors
   - ● illustrators
   - Ⓒ publishers

2. Beatrix Potter liked to draw things from _____.
   - ● nature
   - Ⓑ England
   - Ⓒ other books

3. What are two things Potter drew in *The Tale of Peter Rabbit*?

   A cat; a family of rabbits

4. What other characters were in *The Tale of Peter Rabbit*?

   Flopsy, Mopsy, Cotton-tail, and Peter's

   mother

Write About the Topic
Use the Writing Form to draw and write about what you read.

Draw one of Beatrix Potter's characters. Write to tell about Beatrix Potter's life.

© Evan-Moor Corp. • EMC 3231 • Nonfiction Reading Practice **Beatrix Potter ■ ■ ■ 159**

Page 165

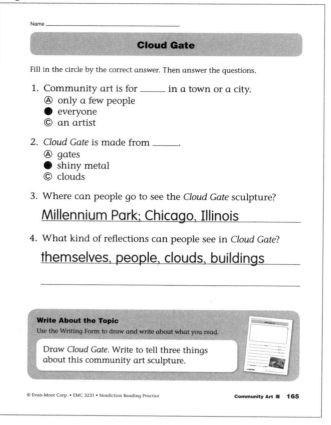

Name _____

Cloud Gate

Fill in the circle by the correct answer. Then answer the questions.

1. Community art is for _____ in a town or a city.
   - Ⓐ only a few people
   - ● everyone
   - Ⓒ an artist

2. *Cloud Gate* is made from _____.
   - Ⓐ gates
   - ● shiny metal
   - Ⓒ clouds

3. Where can people go to see the *Cloud Gate* sculpture?

   Millennium Park; Chicago, Illinois

4. What kind of reflections can people see in *Cloud Gate*?

   themselves, people, clouds, buildings

Write About the Topic
Use the Writing Form to draw and write about what you read.

Draw *Cloud Gate*. Write to tell three things about this community art sculpture.

© Evan-Moor Corp. • EMC 3231 • Nonfiction Reading Practice **Community Art ■ 165**

Page 167

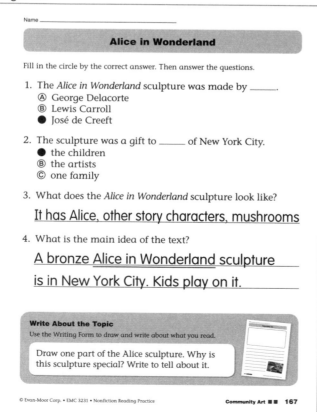

Name _____

Alice in Wonderland

Fill in the circle by the correct answer. Then answer the questions.

1. The *Alice in Wonderland* sculpture was made by _____.
   - Ⓐ George Delacorte
   - Ⓑ Lewis Carroll
   - ● José de Creeft

2. The sculpture was a gift to _____ of New York City.
   - ● the children
   - Ⓑ the artists
   - Ⓒ one family

3. What does the *Alice in Wonderland* sculpture look like?

   It has Alice, other story characters, mushrooms

4. What is the main idea of the text?

   A bronze *Alice in Wonderland* sculpture

   is in New York City. Kids play on it.

Write About the Topic
Use the Writing Form to draw and write about what you read.

Draw one part of the Alice sculpture. Why is this sculpture special? Write to tell about it.

© Evan-Moor Corp. • EMC 3231 • Nonfiction Reading Practice **Community Art ■ ■ 167**

Page 169

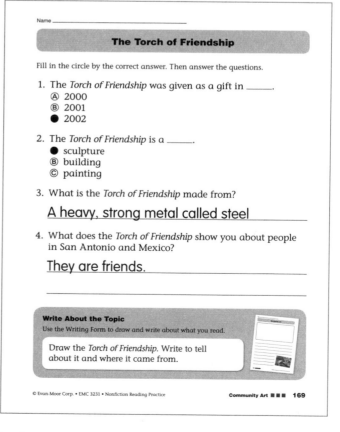

Name _____

The Torch of Friendship

Fill in the circle by the correct answer. Then answer the questions.

1. The *Torch of Friendship* was given as a gift in _____.
   - Ⓐ 2000
   - Ⓑ 2001
   - ● 2002

2. The *Torch of Friendship* is a _____.
   - ● sculpture
   - Ⓑ building
   - Ⓒ painting

3. What is the *Torch of Friendship* made from?

   A heavy, strong metal called steel

4. What does the *Torch of Friendship* show you about people in San Antonio and Mexico?

   They are friends.

Write About the Topic
Use the Writing Form to draw and write about what you read.

Draw the *Torch of Friendship*. Write to tell about it and where it came from.

© Evan-Moor Corp. • EMC 3231 • Nonfiction Reading Practice **Community Art ■ ■ ■ 169**

Page 175

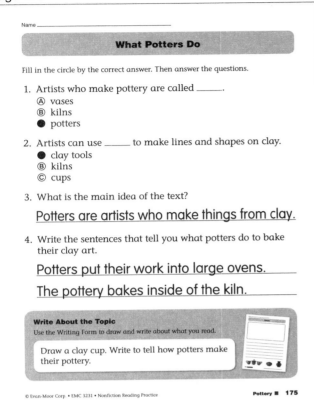

Name _____

What Potters Do

Fill in the circle by the correct answer. Then answer the questions.

1. Artists who make pottery are called _____.
   - Ⓐ vases
   - Ⓑ kilns
   - ● potters

2. Artists can use _____ to make lines and shapes on clay.
   - ● clay tools
   - Ⓑ kilns
   - Ⓒ cups

3. What is the main idea of the text?

   Potters are artists who make things from clay.

4. Write the sentences that tell you what potters do to bake their clay art.

   Potters put their work into large ovens.

   The pottery bakes inside of the kiln.

Write About the Topic
Use the Writing Form to draw and write about what you read.

Draw a clay cup. Write to tell how potters make their pottery.

Pottery ■ 175

Page 177

Name _____

Using a Pottery Wheel

Fill in the circle by the correct answer. Then answer the questions.

1. The potter uses a wheel to make a _____.
   - Ⓐ ball of clay
   - ● clay bowl
   - Ⓒ pottery kiln

2. Potters need _____ to become good artists.
   - Ⓐ luck
   - Ⓑ water
   - ● practice

3. Why can it be hard to use a pottery wheel?

   Sometimes the clay shape can fall in.

4. Why does the potter bake the bowl?

   She bakes the bowl to make it hard.

Write About the Topic
Use the Writing Form to draw and write about what you read.

Draw a clay bowl on a wheel. Write to tell how potters use wheels to make works of art.

Pottery ■ ■ 177

Page 179

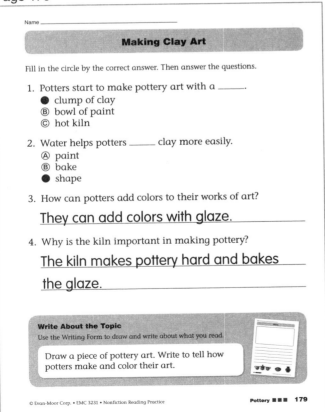

Name _____

Making Clay Art

Fill in the circle by the correct answer. Then answer the questions.

1. Potters start to make pottery art with a _____.
   - ● clump of clay
   - Ⓑ bowl of paint
   - Ⓒ hot kiln

2. Water helps potters _____ clay more easily.
   - Ⓐ paint
   - Ⓑ bake
   - ● shape

3. How can potters add colors to their works of art?

   They can add colors with glaze.

4. Why is the kiln important in making pottery?

   The kiln makes pottery hard and bakes

   the glaze.

Write About the Topic
Use the Writing Form to draw and write about what you read.

Draw a piece of pottery art. Write to tell how potters make and color their art.

Pottery ■ ■ ■ 179

Sample Lesson

Daily 6-Trait Writing GRADE 1

DAY 1

Read the rule aloud to introduce students to the concept of details. Then guide students through the activities. For example:

- **Activity A:** Write the word **detail** on the board. Say the word aloud and have students repeat after you. Then have students trace the word.

- **Activity B:** After reading the sentences for item 1, ask: *What do the sentences say about Ally?* (She is a friend; she has long hair; she smiles.) Say: *These are details about Ally.* Then guide students in reading and underlining the words that tell about these details. Repeat the process for item 2.

Convention: Read the rule aloud. Have students point to the first letter of each name as you read it aloud. Then have them trace the capital letter.

DAY 2

Read the rule aloud and remind students what a detail is. Then guide students through the activities. For example:

- **Activity A:** Direct students to the picture before reading the questions aloud. For question 1, model thinking through the answer. Say: *It looks like Ted spilled his cereal! Is he happy or sad?* (sad) Repeat the process for questions 2 and 3, writing the answers on the board for students to copy.

- **Activity B:** Ask: *What is one thing that Ted has?* Return to questions 1–3 to find possible answers. (e.g., hat, sad face, bowl) Then copy the sentence frame onto the board and model finishing it. For example: *Ted has a sad face.* Have students complete their sentence frames accordingly.

Convention: Read the rule and the sentence aloud. Then read Ted's name aloud as students trace over it. Then have them point to and circle the capital letter.

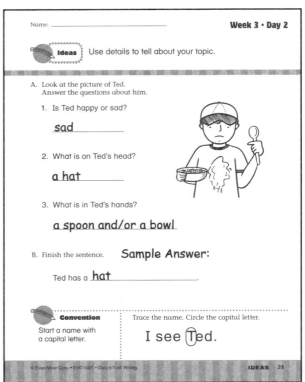

Name: _____   **Week 3 • Day 3**

Ideas Use details to tell about your topic.

A. Look at the picture of the bus.
   Add a detail to the picture.

SCHOOL

Details will vary.

B. Write the detail you added to the picture.

   Sample Answer: kids _____

Convention
Start a name with
a capital letter.

Copy the first and last name.
Start both with a capital letter.

Lisa Wong

Lisa Wong

26 IDEAS   Daily 6-Trait Writing • EMC 6021 • © Evan-Moor Corp.

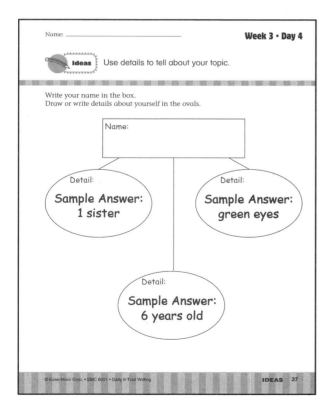

Name: _____   **Week 3 • Day 4**

Ideas Use details to tell about your topic.

Write your name in the box.
Draw or write details about yourself in the ovals.

Name:

Detail:
**Sample Answer:
1 sister**

Detail:
**Sample Answer:
green eyes**

Detail:
**Sample Answer:
6 years old**

© Evan-Moor Corp. • EMC 6021 • Daily 6-Trait Writing   IDEAS 27

DAY 3

Read the rule aloud. Then guide students through the activities. For example:

- **Activity A:** Point to the bus and lead students in brainstorming details in the picture, such as wheels, windows, doors, driver, kids. Then ask: *What detail could we add to the picture?* (e.g., more kids in the windows) Have students add the detail to their pictures.

- **Activity B:** Say: *We drew (detail) in the picture. That is the detail we added.* Then write the word on the board for students to copy.

Convention: Remind students of the rule. Point out the first and last name as you read them aloud. Have students copy them.

DAY 4

Read the rule aloud and explain that today, students will think about details that describe themselves. Then guide students through the activity. For example:

- Copy the web onto the board. Say: *This is a web. We put our topic at the top. We put details about the topic in the ovals underneath.*

- Have students write their names in the box. Say: *You are the topic. Now, let's think of details about you. You could say how old you are, where you live, or what color hair you have.* Write some general details on the board for students to copy. (e.g., 6 years old; brown hair) Model writing the details in the appropriate parts of the web. Circulate and assist students as they fill in their webs.

DAY 5 *Writing Prompt*

- Post this sentence starter: *My name is ___.* Model filling it in with your name. Then post another starter, such as *I am ___ years old.* or *I have ___.* Have students copy the starters and fill them in with their names and details from their webs.

- Remind students to begin their names with a capital letter.

 **Ideas** Details tell about your topic.

A. Trace the word.

detail

B. Read the sentences.
Underline the details.

1. Ally is my friend.
   She has long hair.
   She smiles a lot.

Ally

2. Bananas taste good.
   They are yellow.
   They smell sweet.

bananas

 Convention

Start a name with
a capital letter.

Read the names.
Trace the capital letters.

Ally   Josh

Maria   Sam

 **Ideas** Use details to tell about your topic.

A. Look at the picture of Ted.
   Answer the questions about him.

   1. Is Ted happy or sad?

   _____

   2. What is on Ted's head?

   _____

   3. What is in Ted's hands?

   _____

B. Finish the sentence.

   Ted has a _____.

 Convention

Start a name with
a capital letter.

Trace the name. Circle the capital letter.

I see Ted.

 **Ideas** Use details to tell about your topic.

A. Look at the picture of the bus.
   Add a detail to the picture.

SCHOOL

B. Write the detail you added to the picture.

_____

_____

 Convention

Start a name with
a capital letter.

Copy the first and last name.
Start both with a capital letter.

Lisa Wong

_____

 **Ideas** Use details to tell about your topic.

Write your name in the box.
Draw or write details about yourself in the ovals.

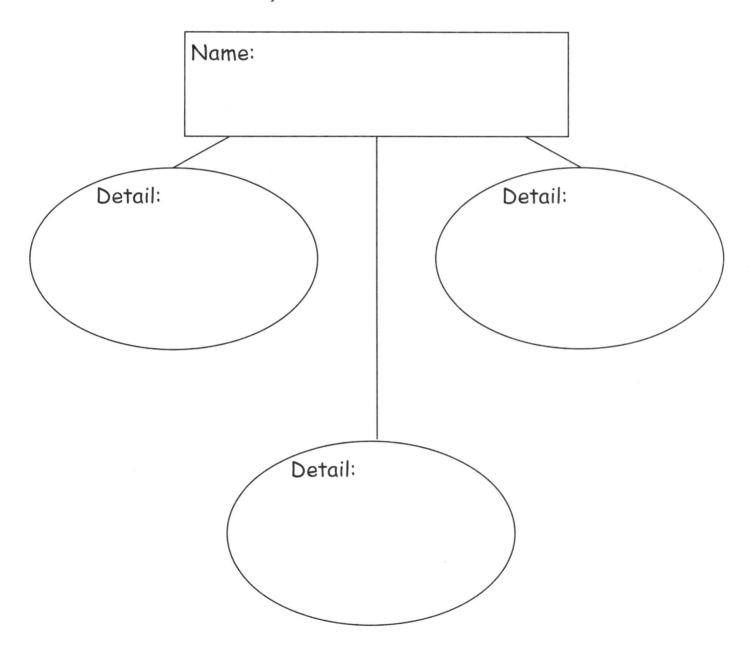

Name:

Detail:

Detail:

Detail:

SKILL SHARPENERS

PreK–6

AWARD-WINNING

"Colorful and fun! **Skill Sharpeners** *has successfully engaged my very easily distracted son. I highly recommend it."*

—Parent, Cambridge, Idaho

Connecting School & Home

Grades PreK–6 *Skill Sharpeners: Reading* provides at-home practice that helps students master and retain skills. Each book in this dynamic series is the ideal resource for programs such as summer school, after school, remediation, school book fairs, and fundraising.

- Activities aligned with national and state standards
- Assessment pages in standardized-test format
- Full-color, charmingly illustrated, and kid-friendly

144 full-color pages.   **www.evan-moor.com/ssh**

The National Parenting Center, Seal of Approval Winner

iParenting Media Awards Outstanding Product

Reading

Activity Book Print

GRADE	EMC
PreK	4527
K	4528
1	4529
2	4530
3	4531
4	4532
5	4533
6	4534

Reading Literary Text

Grades 1–6 Builds strong literary analysis and comprehension skills. Each unit provides literary text in a variety of genres such as myth, folk tale, comedy, realistic fiction, and historical fiction, as well as supporting activities that are easy to scaffold, including close reading, vocabulary, comprehension, literary analysis, and writing.

Includes guided reading levels and correlations to Common Core State Standards and TEKS for easy reference. 144 pages. Correlated to state standards and Common Core State Standards. Federal funding sources: I, 21   **www.evan-moor.com/rlt**

*Grade 1 includes minibooks

Developed for **COMMON CORE**

Reading Literary Text Grade 5

Downloadable home–school connection activities and projects extend learning at home

Teacher's Edition Print

Teacher's Edition E-book

Student Book 5-Pack

Student Book

GRADE	EMC	GRADE	EMC	GRADE	EMC	GRADE	EMC
1	3211	1	3211i	1	6491	1	6481
2	3212	2	3212i	2	6492	2	6482
3	3213	3	3213i	3	6493	3	6483
4	3214	4	3214i	4	6494	4	6484
5	3215	5	3215i	5	6495	5	6485
6	3216	6	3216i	6	6496	6	6486